THE TREA
LITTLE GASPARILLA ISLAND

THE TREASURES OF LITTLE GASPARILLA ISLAND

LLOYD ARTHUR WIGGINS &
ROSEMARY EGERTON LETTS

Library of Congress Control Number: 2013904383
ISBN: Hardcover   978-1-4836-0820-4
               Softcover   978-1-4836-0819-8
               Ebook   978-1-4836-0821-1

This book was printed in the United States of America.

Rev. date: 04/20/2013

To order additional copies of this book, contact:
Xlibris Corporation
1-888-795-4274
www.Xlibris.com
Orders@Xlibris.com
128481

CONTENTS

In memory of
My wife, Nikki, for always being there
Our loyal companion, Napier
Very close friend, George Geier
Ed Strickland, who visited us throughout the world

PROLOGUE

THIS ISLAND'S NAMESAKE is Juan Gomez Gasparilla—or, as he's known today throughout the west coast of Florida, Jose Gaspar. Some think of Gaspar as folklore, while others say he is just a myth. A few locals have stories handed down by ancestors through the ages and say the proof is probably in the United States naval archives, since the pirates were hunted down by the USS *Enterprise* in the early 1800s. They all were either killed or put on trial in New Orleans and subsequently hung, all except for Jose Gaspar. He was alleged to be sixty-five years old and on his last campaign before dividing up the spoils among his cohorts. Rather than get caught, he wrapped himself in the anchor's chain and rope then jumped into the dark blue waters of the Gulf of Mexico to end his life; that was his only way to escape the hangman's noose.

It is believed that Gaspar and his band of thieves and murderers had their haven around Charlotte Harbor. The barrier islands, such as Gasparilla and Little Gasparilla, would have been excellent cover where they could lie in wait behind tall sand dunes or mangroves, searching the Gulf waters for European vessels sailing within sight, carrying gold, silver, and jewels collected from the Americas to take back to their kings and queens or other financiers. Rumor has it that the pirates would slaughter everyone on board the captured ships except for the attractive ladies, who would become concubines of Jose Gaspar. He was a noted womanizer when he was assigned to the court of Charles III as a naval attaché at the age of twenty-seven. He jilted the daughter-in-law of the king for another woman of the court and was about to be arrested on trumped-up charges of treason when he commandeered a Spanish ship, called the *Florida Blanca*, and set sail with a hastily assembled volunteer crew for the Florida straits.

Little Gasparilla had two passes barely navigable for a sailing ship, but not for a man-of-war ship. The much larger pass into Gasparilla Sound was on the south end of Big Gasparilla through the Boca Grande Pass, with its two rivers emptying into the Gulf, flowing through Charlotte Harbor. This proved to be ideal for the crew to hide and pounce on unsuspecting heavily laden sailing ships heading north. Legend has the number of conquered vessels by Gaspar to be over four hundred. Back then, the amount of the bounty was reported to be in excess of thirty million Yankee dollars. Today's count would be in the billions, which would take scores of stolen chests to accommodate the spoils. No treasure of his to this day has ever been found.

I have visited Little Gasparilla most winters for several months during the last seventeen years. On my many walks toward the state park on the north end of the island, I always look wishfully for doubloons washing ashore or a treasure chest sticking out of a tall sand dune while looking for sharks' teeth.

Besides the tangible treasures that may be—in one's wildest dreams, *could* be—found, there are other riches to discover while walking on the sand, be it purely spiritual or just a perfect seashell lying on the shore of Little Gasparilla Island, brought in by the gentle waves.

ACKNOWLEDGMENTS

Julliet Wiggins King (England)
Jimetta Anderson (USA)
Meg Costello (USA)
Susan Wade (USA)
Jim and Jeanette McGill (Scotland)
David and Jacque Bevan (England)

CHAPTER ONE

FINDING LGI

NIKKI AND I, with our oversized black lab, Napier, were getting excited about our annual trip to sunny Florida. The previous night had been Halloween when we had had our first dusting of snow, which added to our longing for warmer weather. The temperate waters of the Gulf of Mexico were calling us! This year was going to be different; Tom and Amber Hurley had visited us on Lake Nottely in the North Georgia Mountains that past summer. One evening, after dinner, they asked us what we did in the winters. Normally, we would go to the Indian Rocks Beach for a month to meet up with Jim and Jeanette McGill from Alyth, Scotland; that was all the four of us could afford.

The Hurleys owned a ranch in Balm, Florida, and were not only friends but also distant cousins of the Wigginses and McLeods on my mother's side of our family. They said that they had a beach house on a barrier island in Southwest Florida just south of Englewood, accessible only by boat and less than a mile from the mainland. It was apparently a little desolate or like having a wide moat around a village. Anyway, they offered us that beach house for the whole winter as long as we were out by the middle of May, when it would be warm enough for them to go down. Florida residents do not go to the beach unless the temperature is in the eighties; they wouldn't swim in the sea if the water wasn't that same temperature.

I couldn't thank them enough; however, Nikki said, "Maybe we could stretch it to six weeks."

And I replied, "Why not three months?"

Nikki reminded me that the antique shop had to be opened on weekends. So I suggested that friends and old employees Cynthia, Tom, Bob, and Betty could work it, as they all had a good record for sales. Nikki still wasn't so sure.

Tom said, "Think about it and let us know. We can move our personal stuff out so that you will have room to put your clothes. The beach house can be yours for the winter. When and if you drive down, stay with us, and we will take you there the next day by car, trailing our boat, to show you how to get on to the island. There is a water taxi at Eldred's Marina on the edge of Gasparilla Bay."

Again I said, "Thank you, but we would like to pay you for us staying there for such a long time."

Amber said, "No way, Lloyd. None of us ever go there from October to the last of May or when school is out."

I said, "What about spring break?"

She said, "Oh my god! On a Florida beach at spring break with college and high school kids—you couldn't pay us to be there. No! Have fun, it's yours."

They left the next day after breakfast for the long drive home. We said, "Good-bye, and thanks, we'll probably see you in early November."

For the next week, we packed and set up a work schedule for the antique shop to be opened weekends, with our accountant paying all fees and taxes to the State of Georgia. We both excitedly agreed that the coming Saturday morning, when we'd be driving through the center of Atlanta on Interstate 75, would be a lot less stressful than a workday.

We were finally on our way, looking adoringly at each other with big smiles and full of overwhelming anticipation. Napier could sense the feelings we had to a point where she edged her nose through and between the seats while still lying down, wanting to be part of our excitement. The Hurleys were expecting us at their ranch house by five that evening, with an extra hour built in for any delays.

After picking up a couple of Egg McMuffins and coffee in Blue Ridge, Nikki drove in the dark to just outside of Cumming, Georgia, ten minutes from the interstate junction of Interstate 75 and Interstate 575 Nikki pulled the Blazer over under an overpass so I could take over the driving to get us through the city. On our way, we both asked ourselves, What is this island that we are going to for at least three months going to be like? We agreed that if we didn't like it after New Year's, we would go back to Blairsville. At that time in our lives, we were trying to build our business, so we just couldn't afford to spend silly money on an extended holiday. Thanks to Tom and Amber, we were able to have it all.

Nikki had phoned Jim and Jeanette about that new area of Florida, and they were as excited as we were at the thought of going to a new beach as long as it was in a warm place. They planned to join us in a few weeks, and we looked forward to seeing them again. They did love Florida—not only for the weather, the beaches, and the cheap food, but also for the fishing equipment and clothes, such as Levi's 501 jeans for Jim (at least half a dozen pairs) which were 50 percent cheaper than in the United Kingdom, not to mention long-sleeved shirts to go with the jeans. Jim would also buy an electric boat motor to use on lakes in Central Scotland where he fished with an angling club. He supplied all his friends by taking one of these engines back every year along with other fishing gear.

Going through Atlanta, talking a mile a minute, we came to the first rest stop on an interstate that cuts off just before Macon connecting to Interstate 75, again shaving off a few miles, to go to the bathrooms and to exercise the dog. Getting ready to hit the road, Nikki said she would take over the driving. She knows I would rather read the paper between our conversations about our exciting future on a Florida barrier island. Napier, being a quiet traveler, would occasionally sneak her head through if she needed a walk or a pet, not knowing we would probably be stopping at the next rest stop; it was good to stretch our legs after a couple of hours driving.

We stopped on the Florida state line on the Georgia side to fill up with cheaper gasoline, enough to get us to the Hurley Ranch, and to give Nikki a rest. I would drive to the next rest stop on the other side of Lake City. That was probably our seventh trip on the same route in the past three years, commuting from North Georgia or Western North Carolina to Southwest Florida. Our feelings for the love of going back home never changed.

We finally got to the state line. We held hands, squeezing lovingly with a shared feeling of euphoria; both of us loved Florida so much and always had. We were now counting the few hours that it would take to pass Riverview, where I was raised on a very small farm, and cross the Alafia River, where swimming had been a welcome relief on the long, hot summer days.

The Lake City rest stop was coming up when Nikki said, "Napier and I have to have a twenty-minute break with some walking-around time."

I thought to myself, *I don't think we passed a rest stop without stopping!* It had worked out well so we could take turns driving.

Back in the Blazer again, while Nikki drove, I was able to take a long-enough nap to wake up while we were pulling into the Ocala rest stop; with renewed energy, I was ready to drive us through Tampa. Soon we were at the Balm cutoff near Sun City, about thirty-five miles south of Tampa. As we drove around the big city to the east, seeing the names of roads and places, it brought back memories of growing up. There were now subdivisions where once cattle meandered over the pastures of ranches and dairy farms.

While daydreaming the miles away, it seemed like, in no time, we were turning off the interstate on to State Road 301. We pulled into Tommy and Amber's place fifteen minutes later. They must have seen us driving up their long driveway, going under the raised entrance with a sign reading that we were now entering the Hurley Ranch. They were outside, waiting, and waved at us enthusiastically. We got out with handshakes and hugs and let Napier out to see chickens running all over the place. That was just too much temptation. She caught one in her mouth, and Nikki screamed at her! I was thinking, *Oh no, I hope this doesn't hurt our friendship.* They were both okay with it, and Napier was immediately put on a leash.

We had a great time with a cookout by their bunkhouse where they kept their barbecue gear under an overhang that was supported by knobbly pine posts. The porch also had roughly cut boards attached to the bunkhouse; it looked like something out of an old Western movie. What a great place to relax after a long, arduous drive! Napier was happy chewing on an old steak bone that Tom had given her. Talking like ranch hands, we told our hosts that we were going to turn in for the night; being weary, sleep was easy to succumb to.

The next morning, Tom took us for a tour of his ranch in an open Jeep through the wetlands where wild hogs were prevalent, then through the vast areas of cattle pastures. We went back to have breakfast before travelling to Englewood to do the big shop that had to include everything we would need for the coming week. Tom said, unfortunately, that they couldn't take us down to the island because of prior commitments, but he told us what to do and where the key was kept under the house. He also phoned Eldred's Marina, so we had a three-hour time frame to get all the shopping completed before catching the water taxi.

We took off for Englewood after once again thanking them for their generosity. Our excitement and anticipation were becoming overwhelming. Finally, we got off the interstate at the Englewood

North Port exit (a road with nothing on it, through low wetlands where the wild hogs frequent the ditches on River Road). Nikki went into the Publix grocery store while I went to buy the grill and the charcoal at Kmart to save time, then I joined her with my own cart to load up mainly with water and Coca-Cola. We kept passing each other in the aisles, happily shopping, with a little pressure to be at the marina's water taxi on time. Once we finished the mammoth shop, the trick was to squeeze it all into the back of our SUV and leave just enough room for Napier.

Off through the small town of Englewood south on Placida Road, we arrived at Eldred's Marina ten minutes later. The look on our faces must have been priceless because we thought we had to be in the wrong place. A tin-covered shanty could not be a marina! It looked more like a backwoods fish camp one would find on a river in the Ozarks. When we went inside to pay for the three months' parking and the water taxi fare, a smiling young girl greeted us. She welcomed us to Eldred's Marina and said that her name was Ruthy. After paying what we thought was a reasonable fee to park for that length of time, the water taxi fare of twenty dollars each struck us as expensive. But on reflection, when we considered all our gear that had to be transported, we felt it wasn't so bad.

Our boat captain was Sam, Ruthy's brother, a young man in his twenties with shaggy red hair, no shoes, and a pleasant manner. He had a kind of teasing talk that made me think Sam was a real-life Tom Sawyer down to his bare toes. We all loaded up the taxi, and Sam steered it through the channel; he pointed to an island we could see through a canopy of trees on the other side of the Bay about a mile away. We had noticed, earlier, bumper stickers on trucks at the marina that read: "Do Not Ban Nets."

Sam explained that the government stopped the gillnetting of mullet for their roe, which was then exported to the Orient. He was upset by the government preventing that way of making money and the interference of the Clinton administration. I definitely was not a fan of the president; however, I quietly thought that they were protecting the fish from being overharvested. If I had shared my concerns, it would have shown me as a left-leaning environmentalist wacko, so I decided that some things were better left alone—especially in the middle of a body of water!

Sam then started talking to Nikki. He was absolutely intrigued by her posh accent. He commented, "You should have been a schoolteacher, ma'am."

Her reply to him was "It's strange you should say that, Sam. I was a teacher in England and Florida in the sixties and seventies."

"You look way too young to be retired," Sam adoringly added.

"Thank you, Sam. Lloyd and I are now antique dealers, which allows us to travel without time restraints, but more importantly, we love working together." Nikki added, "Now, Sam, spending three months on an island with him may be our biggest test yet!"

Sam laughed, saying, "You guys will do just fine."

The boat proceeded slowly alongside the island in order to reduce its wake. It ensured that we wouldn't make waves that would rock the boats tied up to the numerous docks at the end of each lane or the docks in front of small homes built on low stilts and the few older homes directly on the ground. The majority of these places looked like they were built in the sixties or seventies; there were no modern-looking homes. The dock numbers were getting higher the farther we traveled, and the delight was showing on our faces the closer we got to dock 88. Sam said, "Here we are," as he pulled alongside our port of call.

After unloading all our gear and provisions, including gallons of springwater covering most of the dock area, we picked up the luggage holding our important possessions to take with us to look for the house we would be living in for the next few months. Stepping onto Peacock Lane with Nikki and Napier and walking toward the Gulf of Mexico was amazing! The lane was sandy, with seashells and exposed roots crossing the path. There were lots of palm trees, which led to a canopy of sea grape and Brazilian pepper trees along with very large Australian pines. I was overwhelmed and bursting inside with such a euphoric feeling; it was similar to falling in love. I just hoped that Nikki would like that part of Florida even just a little. I had definitely come back home after spending fourteen years overseas.

When we got through the canopy of trees, the lane opened up where we could see six houses on both sides with the roaring sound of the Gulf as a backdrop. Tom's house was the first on the right, with a cute front porch and gray asbestos siding. Pine needles covered the roof from the huge tree in the front yard—or garden, as Nikki would call it. The windows were cloudy with grime and a saltlike film. It was not exactly a posh condo, which was our usual winter holiday rent. For some wonderful reason, I liked that place a lot better. It was so much nicer than being in a high-class area where a dog could not be walked for the lack of spare land. Last year, we had to take Napier by car miles away from the beach to give him his exercise without trespassing.

Going up the steps, we set our luggage down on the porch; from there we could see the water, with waves breaking onto the shore. I went under the house to get the key. Tom and Amber's beach house was on stilts, and at one time, it was possible to walk without stooping underneath, but now, with added sand from the Gulf, one had to bend quite a bit to get under it. The key was where it was supposed to be: on top of a large post.

When we opened the door, there was an odor of damp, humid mustiness that quickly engulfed us. We looked for a fan to help air it out while we opened the doors and windows (those that would open without being pried up because they were the old sash type that no longer had weights and ropes attached) to give the beach house a good blow through. The electrics were turned on at the main breaker box. We noticed the rust had started to eat into it on the outside, but we could see it was still safe. However, a more disturbing problem was the water pump—it simply would not kick in!

We were now a little concerned about staying that night if we couldn't get water to flush the toilet. The water pump was under the house; we inspected the electrical wires and found them to be all right, but the pump was seized up through rust accumulation. I went upstairs to tell Nikki and found her out on the porch, having a cigarette in the hope of relaxing. A few minutes later, she saw a man walking by toward the Bay. Nikki called me to come outside to ask him if he knew someone that could help us.

I called as I walked in his direction to explain our dilemma. I introduced myself to him and explained our problem; he said that his name was Bob Hill and that he was a builder on the island. Yes, he could help us as he just happened to have a new pump in his workshop. He said, "Give me a few minutes to gather the tools needed, and I will have you water within the hour."

While Bob was gone, we were both emotionally relieved; fate was being kind to us. Thank God for Bob being in the right place at the right time. When he came back to fix the problem, he mentioned that he was getting Mr. Geier's house, farther down the lane, ready for him to move in for the winter. Mr. Geier could be arriving anytime within the next couple of weeks. We also asked Bob to take a look at the electrics while the pump work was being done; we finally started moving our shopping into the house.

While Nikki cleaned up the bedrooms, bathroom, and the kitchen area, I went back on the dock to see mullet jumping, with ospreys and pelicans diving into the Bay. Even a dolphin was feeding on the mullet. What a wonderfully quiet, peaceful, and serene part of the world, without manmade noise. There was a pull cart under the small house on the Bay next to our dock, which I was able to borrow to haul half our goods up at a time. It was tough, pulling it through the sand, but a small price to pay to be able to stay there—especially that night, with all our emotions going through the roof.

After Bob the builder finished up, Nikki said, "How wonderful." Three hundred dollars later, we could not thank him enough for rescuing us. When he left, we went inside to put everything away. Nikki gave me a hug, saying, "I am so glad, darling, for you. I can see on your face how much you want this place to work out for us."

Trying to convey the feeling I had when I first stepped onto the island was hard; it was difficult to explain such emotion in just a few words. We both worked feverishly hard to finish putting everything away, from clothes to food, and we were also trying to fit all perishables in the small fridge/freezer. The cleaning was hastily done so we could be on the beach at sunset.

Nikki said, "Lloyd, I found another box of clothes on the side steps of the front porch you will have to deal with."

So off to the bedroom I went, to sort out still more of our stuff. Then we finally had everything put away (we hoped). The bedding was changed, our drinks were poured, and we were ready for our first sunset on Little Gasparilla Island (which we very quickly learned to refer to it as LGI). We looked both ways on the beach without seeing another person. Then it hit us: we could be the only ones there when darkness fell. A little sense of vulnerability started to sink in.

CHAPTER TWO

 **A DOG'S ISLAND**

NAPIER WAS CHASING sandpipers by the water's edge when Nikki noticed one of them had only one leg, and she was saying, "Ah, poor little thing." The sandpiper would take a few hops before flying away with the others. The birds would be flying and squawking around Napier in protest and then land behind her only yards away.

We toasted each other for being fortunate enough to be on such a beautiful beach, as anyone who had been on a South Florida beach where the sands are blindingly white would understand. With her hand in mine, we both stood taking in everything that made up the gorgeous view: the sun going down, a few dolphins cruising by, pelicans flying in formation (breaking only when diving for fish), and to complete the experience, a hint of salty brine on our lips. Napier began to tire of chasing strange birds she had never seen before and went in for a swim to cool off. That was in stark contrast to where we stayed in the past years at Indian Rocks, where dogs were not allowed on the beaches.

The sun was going down quickly. We noticed that, at first, it took forever to fall, but as it got closer to the horizon, the sun seemed to speed up its descent into the water. As we started to go up the lane where the beach started—or ended, according to one's perspective from the Bay or from the Gulf—we saw a round house on the beach beside our lane, which had a large deck with chairs stacked in the back and a large white table in the front. It looked like a very inviting place to sit. The house was shuttered up, and the deck hung over part of the beach. I paused and considered maybe going up there. I did refrain when Nikki said it would be bad form to use someone else's property without permission. However, we both thought it would be a nice place to watch whatever was going on.

Then it was time to go back to the house to feed the dog and light the charcoal to cook steaks for our first meal on LGI. While the coals were getting started, we had a glass of wine on the porch. The swing looked like a fun place to rest until we both noticed that the chains holding it up were very rusty, which made us a little apprehensive of it taking our weight. We decided to bring out a couple of chairs and play it safe.

After supper, we took Napier on a walk toward the Bay with a couple of flashlights, going through the tree lined lane. After we had walked through the overhang of trees close to the house, the lane's white sand showed up with the light of the moon. In the dark, we could hear fish jumping all over the Bay, while the baitfish were noisily flipping on top of the water. Sitting on the edge, shining our light into the dark waters, we could pick out large snook and tiny sea horses snuggling up to the dock where we were sitting.

It was so nice being close to Nikki with Napier leaning up against me. The lights across the Bay lined the shore from Boca Grande Bridge to the upmarket condos of Placida. Our excitement outweighed the tiredness that was setting in. Nikki suggested we consider going back to walk on the beach before turning in, which was fine by me, but Napier had another idea. She waded into the Bay before we could stop her. We didn't really mind as we would let her go into the surf to wash off the smelly Bay water.

Flashlights were not needed on the beach, so we dropped them off on the porch before continuing on the few steps toward the sea and coaxed Napier into the Gulf by throwing a stick to fetch. We had to walk under two houses with their front supports standing in a few feet of water. To avoid wading in deep, we walked around the posts at the rear of the houses. It was a good thing they were built on stilts as that allowed us to walk on the beach. We were both glad that one of these wasn't Tom and Amber's place. I think it would have been a little scary, having the waves lapping against the supports. However, the bonus was that one could fish from the front deck!

Walking hand in hand summed up the closeness we had felt all day, especially as everything had worked out after the water pump was replaced—which allowed us to stay overnight, after all. Being on a strange island, cut off from the modern world, Nikki and I were able to share our personal thoughts and feelings after nearly thirty years of marriage and all the everyday things that can get in the way. There's no way of knowing what causes people to be moved by different circumstances.

Getting back to the house, we washed the sand off the dog. The well water was brown and smelly, but at least it did the trick. After toweling the dog down, it was time to go to sleep while listening to the waves crashing onto the shore.

Waking up early the next morning to let the dog out and put the coffee on, I turned the TV on to catch up on the news. The reception was so snowy; I couldn't hear or make out what was on the screen. Oh well, three months without it would be a test—to have no commercial entertainment, just the great outdoors for amusement. After taking a cup of coffee to Nikki, Napier and I went for a walk on the beach. Still, there was no one in sight for miles.

The island, with its lack of police or human activity, had been an ideal landing place for Cubans fleeing the Castro regime, and it still is today. I grew up on the outskirts of Tampa where there was a large number of first- and second-generation Cubans who had successfully disseminated into a mixed society and brought with them an attitude of "tomorrow will suffice if some task was not accomplished today." I enjoy the Cuban way of dealing with normal, everyday living as well as the way they use the different spices in their varied cooking, using all kinds of fish and meat from deviled crab to tasty paella dishes.

Little Gasparilla Island was also used as a landing area for our planes searching for German submarines during World War II. Pulling military duty there must have been a dream posting, escaping the harsh fighting in Asia or Europe. The area is so close to Boca Grande where tarpon fishing has always been a sport that attracted thousands of anglers throughout the States, and it would have added to the enjoyment of being stationed there. There are restaurants on the mainland displaying tarpon scales (some larger than half dollars) on trophies of mahogany shields dating back to the turn of the century. Tarpon tournaments are still staged in the large Boca Grande Pass, lasting for a few weeks every year toward the start of the summer holiday period.

I went back to see if Nikki was up and ready for breakfast. We toasted our bread to take out on the porch; it was a little too cool to wear shorts, unusual for that time of year. We were still enjoying ourselves, knowing how much colder it was where we had come from a couple of days earlier. Eating our toast and drinking coffee, the topic of discussion was about exploring the island that morning. Neither of us could get over the strong, pleasing smell of the Gulf. It was so salty, with a cleansing feeling to the nose. The first thing was to walk the dog toward the dock, hoping she would go into the woods to "spend a penny," as the English call going to the bathroom. We passed the large house on the right where Peacock Lane met Grande Avenue when Napier noticed two dogs in the yard. She rushed over to meet them, with us telling her no. The lady living there was doing some gardening and said that it was okay. She stated that Bonnie and Jasper were noisy, but harmless. We introduced ourselves to her.

She said, "My name is June." She listened with interest to our three-month plan to be there on the island. June was an attractive lady with a lovely demeanor. One of her dogs, a slightly overweight long-haired Scotty, was barking at Napier, with June saying, "Hush, Bonnie, be nice like Napier." Jasper was a dirty-whitish little poodle with a row of top teeth protruding just a little.

Nikki said good-bye to June and myself to go back to the house as Napier and I kept walking toward the Bay. The tide was high, making the only boat tied to the dock a little too high, causing the ropes to be taut. The name of the boat, a twenty-two-foot Aqua sport, was the *Sandwitch*, and it probably belonged to June since, apart from us, she was the only other person on the lane. Mullet were jumping everywhere, around the docks, and by the mangroves across to our left. A pair of dolphins was feeding and blowing loudly. They came within a few feet of where Napier and I stood; gulls were feeding on small bits of fish left by the dolphins, and pelicans and ospreys were diving in to feed as well. The Bay was just bursting with activity!

We hurriedly walked back to the house to get Nikki so that she could come and see what was happening. The three of us hurried back and sat on the dock's edge to watch for a while; Nikki was really intrigued by dolphins playing and feeding. As we walked back, June was still in her garden. Napier went over to get a drink out of her dogs' water bowl under a spigot, with both of us saying, "No, Napier, that's not your water."

June said, "Anytime she wants a drink, let her have it. Besides, I don't have to lug water from the mainland. My first plan was to put in a reverse-osmosis system when my house was built, so if you guys need water, just help yourselves."

Both of us quietly thought we couldn't take such a liberty, even though we got along famously with June. Nikki invited her and her dogs to our place for sunset, thinking that the more time they spent with Napier, maybe the barking would subside. "I'll be there," June said, and we replied, "Great! See you about five thirty."

We walked back to the beach house and felt good about meeting someone so nice who was also a local who would know the ins and outs of the island. The morning was going by quickly, with us really doing almost nothing. We looked forward to our cup of tea while sitting again on the front porch with the Gulf in the background. After tea, Napier went down the steps; she wanted another walk. We all went back to the beach to look for shells while Napier swam in the surf when she was not agitating the birds. Nikki spotted the one-legged sandpiper again, feeding on the water's edge, and told Napier to walk in the other direction. She felt sorry for the little bird not being like the others.

It was time to go back for a late lunch, then to take a nap while Nikki did a crossword puzzle or finished the book she had started in Georgia. After an hour of sleeping, Nikki heard me getting up; she had a cup of tea waiting on the porch with a cinnamon bun. I could not believe Nikki was actually enjoying an island without the amenities of shopping or going out to eat, especially while on a holiday. She was saying how relaxed she was, enjoying the peacefulness. We sauntered off to the beach to look for shells to add to Tom and Amber's collection lining the wall on the porch against the house. Shelling was very good, and there were so many to look through piled up on the beach, with the waves bringing them in. Soon our bucket was full of treasures of the shore, and then it was time to go back to get ready for June, Bonnie, and Jasper.

The shower's brown water seemed to make us smell more like sulfur or something worse rather than soap! We were told that all wells on the island were as shallow as five feet because the water table was not far under the sandy soil. We were also told by Bob Hill that we needed to move the well hole under a tall sand drift since the more sand, the better it was as it got filtered as the rainwater drained through it. A five-foot drift on top of the soil would be ideal, but since we would have to go through someone's property to get better water, it seemed fruitless to even think about it. June was coming up the lane as we were going to sit outside on the deck.

She was thrilled to be invited for drinks and snacks even though she brought her own drink, saying to us that was what island people did. She told us about a T-shirt of hers that read "You float it, You tote it." We were all responsible for taking our garbage off the island since there was no trash pickup. We had lots of questions about Little Gasparilla to ask her. She wanted to know if we had walked to the state park, about a twenty-minute walk north, where we could collect shells on the way. She added that there were bathroom facilities and freshwater piped from the mainland and a large pavilion for picnicking, and if you went there by boat, there were several well-maintained docks. We said that we hadn't been anywhere, not knowing where to go. She also told us that there was a nice little library behind Hoot's house on the Bay, close to Don Fowler's house, the resident real estate agent. That was extremely good news for Nikki, who was an avid reader, going through at least two books a week. June also added that Don Fowler had a lime tree that gave forth plenty of fruit for making drinks or baking. If we were really adventurous, there was a restaurant about an hour's walk north of the park on Palm Island where they had killer shrimp and crab cakes to go with their famous drinks or iced tea. We were given lots of information to keep us busy for the next few days.

The sun was almost down, so it was time to take ourselves and the dogs to the beach to watch it set. Afterward, we walked back to the house, with June saying good night and that it had been fun as she continued down the lane to her place followed by her dogs. We had to get our dog fed as well as ourselves. While Nikki was fixing the meals, I poured her a glass of Chardonnay while my drink was going to be a cold Cabernet; that would be our first meal on the table inside. Our decision was that the following morning, after breakfast, we would look for Hoot's library; however, that night, there was still time for one more walk on the beach to get Napier some exercise. We could see for miles both ways, and as far as we could tell, there were no lights or signs of life. We were able to keep Napier out of the water by taking her high on the beach and not letting her amble down to the surf. It was a small miracle to keep that lab out of any kind of water.

Darkness was falling, which meant it was time for us to head home to clean up the kitchen before going to bed. We anticipated more discoveries the next day. What a wonderful day it had been, and it had gone by so fast. We were at the point where we had to ask each other what day it was since we had no places to be and no more appointments to keep. Time doesn't mean much on an island.

We went to bed talking more and more about how we were enjoying being together, knowing for now that time was not passing us by. Napier was likely snoring with the sound of waves breaking outside; sleep came quickly with added weary bliss.

Napier woke up just after five; we walked to the Bay with flashlight in hand for her to stretch her legs before breakfast. I was standing on the dock in the blackness, with fish jumping and a couple of dolphins feeding on them with an eerie sound of loud blows coming from below. Their blowholes and even louder splashing could make it seem scary to someone who didn't know what was causing the commotion, especially in the pitch-black night. I was sitting on the dock with my feet dangling close to the dark water, not seeing what was swimming in it. Later, I would take a plastic chair there to leave tied to the fish-cleaning station so that it wouldn't get blown away. With the chair on the dock, it would be really enticing to fish, so the next trip to Englewood might mean a trip to Walmart for some tackle with the spinning rod and artificial lures, along with some guidance from their fishing expert. Napier was now ready to go back for breakfast.

Nikki was up making coffee while asking, "Where have you two been?" We were full of our adventures that morning; Napier kept quiet, looking at her food bowl. We took our coffee out on the porch where the dog was to be fed. It was still a little dark, but not as much as earlier. We went in for another coffee, Nikki pouring while I toasted bread.

She said, "Could we go to the library after we have our breakfast?"

"Sure," I said, "but I would like to drop off a plastic chair that is stored under the house to leave on our dock."

After an hour or so, we headed for the library, passing June's house where Bonnie was out in her yard, barking, obviously telling Napier to keep off her territory. June was yelling out the back door for Bonnie to hush up in her distinctive Texas drawl. We dropped the chair off at the dock before continuing to the library, crossing the half a dozen properties on the Bay with riparian rights; it wasn't trespassing, as strange as it seemed to us. June had given us good directions where to find Hoot's house; following the Bay's edge would get us there eventually.

No boats were to be seen tied up to more than a dozen docks. The only boats on any docks were the two at the end of our lane serving another dozen houses. It was difficult to understand why no one was there to enjoy the warm weather in November! We were amazed that there was hardly anyone there.

Hoot's house was pretty easy to find, being a little different than the others. It was sort of a detached cottage and served as the island library. When we opened the door, it was a bit dark and musty smelling, and we found the light switch to see children's school desks with children's books on them; the walls were lined with bookcases full of all types of subjects, with mysteries being the most prevalent choices, which suited Nikki as that was her favorite read. I always liked reading about rural Florida (except for the yearling, because it was a little sad). My choice would be happy endings since Florida, with its white beaches and endless sunshine, is a feel-good place to live in.

Nikki was having fun; all her most-liked authors were represented there. After choosing our books, we were off to have a cup of tea back at the beach house. On the way, a gopher turtle was very slowly crossing the sandy Grande Avenue Lane. Napier didn't know what to make of this huge bulbous thing that was just barely moving along. It had been twenty-five years since we had seen one of these creatures that should be protected by all Floridians. We waited until he or she was completely back into the trees before moving on.

Back with a cup of tea on the porch, we were leafing through our books, which we didn't have to check out because, of course, there was an honor system in place. We would also donate the books we brought with us when we took another trip there in a week or two's time. We had an early lunch, which meant a nap afterward for me to catch up on sleep that had been interrupted really early that morning. Nikki said she was going to visit June after lunch to thank her for telling us about the library.

I slept for over an hour, and then I joined Nikki on the porch after making us a cup of tea. She really enjoyed visiting June and had been given a tour of her house. She had a view of the Gulf from the room on top—a widow's watch, built in the old days by sea captains living on the coast throughout the world. So June incorporated the extra room so she could get a view while not actually being on the waterfront. We were invited for supper that night with Napier to keep her dogs company and were told not to bring anything, including drinks. She needed to use up a lot of provisions before the expiration date, she said. We were expected around six o'clock for drinks, so there was time to go to the beach for a walk; Napier was happy.

CHAPTER THREE

 **SHELLING**

NIKKI PICKED UP Amber's plastic bucket off the porch full of shells she had to empty, as she wanted to collect some more. The surf during the night had brought in loads of new bounty for us to sift through. My favorite ones were the large, elongated, fanned-out, sea scallop-type shells. Some were extremely old and had oxidized while being bleached by the sun and resembled smooth mother-of-pearl in quite long lengths. Nikki was always looking for small perfect clamshells with ridges similar to the Shell Oil logo in different colors. Napier was also having a good time swimming when not chasing sandpipers.

There were very few people on the beach, just a walker or two with their dogs. The water felt a little cold while I waded in, hoping to take a dip. After a few minutes of trying to get the nerve, I finally dived in to get used to the chilly water. Napier swam out to me with paws stretched out in front of her, doing doggie paddle. I had to be careful not to get clawed while playing with her. Diving through the waves helped with the cold-water shock while filling my nose up, and there was a taste, almost like a raw oyster without the meat, in the back of my throat. We were both salty and sandy enough to have to be hosed off once we got back to the house.

Nikki was farther down the beach, so we ran through the low part of the surf to catch up with her. The bucket was pretty full;

only special shells would now be added on our stroll back. What was really surprising to us was that there were no trash or litter bins to be seen. The odd piece of litter that was about probably blew out from a boat rather than someone leaving their litter on the beach.

Nikki said, "You two are covered with sand and are in need of a shower."

We had probably been on the beach for over an hour, and she told me that after we get cleaned up, she would have a cup of tea ready to go with the cinnamon buns.

I always looked forward to a sweet roll after a shower, especially during our afternoon teatime. Nikki and I could relax before going out to dinner by doing a little reading outside. We gave Napier her supper and had time to walk her down the lane again. After waiting awhile for the dog, we could hear her rustling through the thick undergrowth and called for her to hurry up and come out.

We finally arrived at June's house where she was waiting for us by the door, and she led the way upstairs. A variety of scrumptious hors d'oeuvres was served with different wines—what a treat! Talking about the area with June, we were curious as to why Palm Island was called an island when it was not a true island like Boca Grande (Big Gasparilla). She told us that a monster hurricane in about 1960 called Donna closed in all three islands—Palm, Don Pedro, and Little Gasparilla. There was a pass between LGI and Don Pedro where the state park now is. Originally, boats could go out to the Gulf between the two islands, but now they have to channel down Gasparilla Bay through a small pass at the southern end of LGI next to Boca Grande. June added that now there was an uninterrupted seven-mile beach to walk on. In the old days, one could use jeeps on the way up to Palm Island, but now no vehicles were allowed, mainly to protect the nesting sea turtles.

"That is a good thing," she said, and we all agreed. Why would you drive when you could walk or go by boat and enjoy the beautiful surroundings?

The story about Hurricane Donna brought back memories; I told them I was fifteen when she blew through Riverview, taking our roof off. Rain pelted us in our beds at three in the morning, so Mom gathered us all up to walk to my sister Prissy's house, which was made of concrete block while ours was more like a stick house or a framed building. The trek normally would take a few minutes, but that night, it was a struggle in the blackness to pick our way through fallen branches and trees with only one flashlight between us. The sound of the howling wind and the power lines crackling while arching off the ground for several feet on Bloomingdale Road was a little unsettling for all of us kids. We stayed upright by all of us linking arms in the strong wind until reaching Prissy's front door, and then we all faced flat against the house as Mom was knocking on the door, waiting for either her or Jerry to let us in. Prissy put on the coffeepot for the grown-ups and made beds wherever there was space in the front room, away from windows, for her brother and sisters. After sleeping on the floor for a couple of hours, we woke up to calm but rainy weather and could see power lines still jumping as they sparked on the road. Huge pine trees were pushed over in twenty-foot swathes as far as we could see.

June said that we were all very lucky for not walking in one of the stronger wind paths that could have done so much damage to us. Looking back now, I agreed, but as a teenage boy, the thought of danger never entered my head that night—only to anticipate what we would see in the morning from the destruction the winds and rain had done. Nikki said she never knew or had heard me speak about that episode of my life. There are certain things one blocks out, if needed, in their past to have an attitude of hoping that it was a once-in-a-lifetime phenomenon. No one could believe such a storm could have the force to close passes or open them up; after living through one, I was around to see firsthand the next day's devastation. That night, the memories were flooding back!

The most devastating thing about the storm was that almost 50 percent of our farmland was under at least three feet of water. The cows, pigs, and chickens somehow made it to the part of the farm that was higher and somewhat dry. We were very lucky not to lose any livestock. School was cancelled for over a week since all the major roads were littered with fallen trees. Today, that hurricane would have been a category 4 or 5, and there were no government forces back then to help people. All the neighbors would pitch in to fix the most important things first, such as roofs or windows, then the cleanup would start, which would last months, sawing up the fallen trees before hauling them to the burn piles by hand or with the tractor.

We sat down to a lovely meal with all the finery you would find in an uptown restaurant. During the meal, June was telling us all about her friends and neighbors on the island—specifically on Peacock Lane, all of whom she described as "nice as can be" in her Texas drawl. One experience with her island neighbors was on a trip the previous winter to Wyoming with Ed and Louise Sasser, who lived right on the Bay at the end of the lane. After flying into the Jackson Hole Airport, they all went snowmobiling on a five-day trek. We thought that at June's age, that was a marvelous endeavor. One of her many interesting jobs had been as an airline pilot in World War II, ferrying planes in the USA, women not being allowed back then to fly on combat missions. We decided we would love to know more about this courageous lady. June still traveled annually to exotic places with her daughter Judy, who visited her often there on LGI.

After coffee and tasty homemade dessert, we thanked her for her hospitality and the fantastic food and said good night. Walking back to the house without a light wasn't too bad except for not seeing Napier as she ventured off the lane to investigate noises in the trees. We called Napier back so we could go home for some much-needed sleep. As we were going to sleep, we talked about maybe going to the state park after breakfast to see if we could replenish our drinking and cooking water supply by taking a few jugs to fill up.

We were up early for breakfast to get ready to explore the state park. After our toast and coffee, we were on our way, following June's instruction to walk to the right up the beach. The first hindrance we came to was a large stilt home sticking out partially into the Gulf, making us navigate under the structure farther back toward its rear pilings because the tide was in. We wondered how long it would take before that house would be taken away by the waves. Then we continued down where we could see where the separation had been at one time from LGI and Don Pedro Island. The Bay was the closest to the Gulf there, creating a marshy area, and just past the cut-in was a ten-foot sand dune or mini cliff that ran for over one hundred yards. The roof of the pavilion in the park could now be seen. We were wondering if a ranger would be on duty and what that would do for our chances of filling the four-gallon water jugs. There were two sets of steps going up and through the pavilion, and the other set of steps passed a shower and bathrooms with a water cooler outside. No one was there, which gave us time to fill our vessels using the water cooler. It was a slow process, but worth it, and it was nice to know where water could be gotten when we ran low.

We set our water on a picnic table to walk farther into the park to look for the docks, which were supposed to be on the Bay. They were a really nice setup, with mooring for several boats separated by walkways. The dock was well built and was superbly maintained, like the rest of Don Pedro State Park. We started walking back, with two jugs hanging off my shoulders by Napier's leash and carrying two in my hands so Nikki wouldn't have to lug any heavy gallon jugs back down the beach to our house. She would also be able to look for shells and coral, of which we had found a large piece on the way up.

On the way back, Nikki told me that some of our staples were in need of being replenished soon, especially bread and milk. It was still early enough for me to call Sam to see if he had any pickups or drop-offs later that morning. We strolled a little faster, hoping to catch Sam at the marina.

When we got back, Nikki made us a cup of tea as I called Eldred's. Sam was coming to the island to drop someone off at 10:00 a.m. on a rental home a little to the south, and he would pick me up soon after that, which gave me a half hour to be on dock 88.

CHAPTER FOUR

 GOING TO ENGLEWOOD

NIKKI KISSED ME good-bye and asked if I had my wallet and car keys. I had everything I needed, and I picked up a couple of empty boxes for hauling back canned goods while grabbing four empty water jugs to fill up at the Publix distilled-water machine, plus the two large bags of trash to dispose of on the other side. Nikki decided to help me take everything down to the dock after dropping the jugs a couple of times, and we wanted to be a little early so as not to miss the water taxi. Sam could be early, as he often was; luckily he was always patient. He pulled alongside as I walked up the walkway; we loaded up, and Sam asked Nikki if she was going across. She told Sam that someone had to hold down the fort.

Sam replied, "You have a moat around the fort to keep undesirables out."

She said, "They could call the water taxi for passage over."

Sam replied, "We do a good job of screening all possible passengers."

This brought a chuckle to all of us, and then we took off for the marina. On the other side, I loaded up my SUV before going in to pay for dumping trash in the dumpster as well as the taxi fare. While paying Ruthy, I asked if it were possible to book passage back around 2:00 p.m.

She said, "Sam has someone else to take over at three this afternoon if that would work for you, Lloyd."

"Yes," I said. This would give me time to look for a fishing rod at Kmart or Walmart.

It did feel good to be back in the Blazer again. After all my stops for different types of shopping, I was back at Eldred's at two thirty with fishing rod in hand. The other passenger was just pulling in as I unloaded everything on the dock next to the taxi. Sam wasn't around, so I asked an older, very slender man standing on the dock next to the water taxi if he had seen our driver. He introduced himself as Harry, and he would be taking us over, without explaining where Sam was. We were ready to go after paying our fare to him. He was a pleasant sort, but there wasn't much conversation between all of us.

Harry dropped off the other guy first about halfway toward dock 88. I believe it was around Marsh Street, toward the middle of the island. Then we headed to the south end again, still without any conversation. I thought to myself that by making it to my dock just after three, it might give me some time for a nap once the shopping was in the house. I borrowed the plastic cart again from the little house on the left and thought I could make it in one big, heavy trip if it was stacked as high as possible. It was a struggle, pulling it through the sandy lane, which was extremely thick and soft, but I was determined to make it, just in case the owners were coming in for the weekend and needed the cart. Nikki put things away as I trotted up the steps with everything except the water, which we left on the porch in the shade. We used up water so quickly that it didn't have time to turn bad.

Nikki noticed a rotisserie chicken for supper with potato salad as a side. "Good," she said. "We can start the weekend off by taking it easy."

I asked her to take the cart back when she said, "Take a nap, Lloyd. I will walk Napier at the same time and leave the cart under the little gray house."

After a quick shower, I was really tired and ready for a well-deserved nap. It felt good to lie down to rest, knowing we didn't have to go to the mainland for at least another week. The water would have to be replenished within the week by going to the park, which was a fun walk with Napier. I was awakened by Nikki bringing in a cup of tea, saying laughingly, "Darling, are you rested enough to stay up until maybe nine tonight?"

Smiling, I was saying at the same time, "I really don't know as that seems pretty late for islanders, but I will give it my best shot!"

"Oh, Nikki, I forgot to tell you. A few boats have come in probably for the weekend, and it may be the last of the good weather for a while." It was hard for us to know what the weather was going to do since we had no TV to keep us up to date with the climate or to know when cold fronts would be moving down from the frozen North.

I said, "Let's go to the dock to see if any new people have arrived with their boats, and we can walk the dog at the same time."

On our dock, there were no signs of new life around, but I anticipated that the next day might bring something. Who knows? There actually could be new people to meet.

We were walking back to get ready for sunset, talking about the kids and how their studies were going in Britain. We were both relieved that they were in two fairly safe cities, close to many of our friends so that they could visit on weekends if the feeling for a Sunday roast or being with family came over them, and Nikki had many cousins not far away if Julliet or Jonathan needed them. She believed this was a part of her feeling at ease with life because of Jonathan's history with drugs and alcohol. He was going to the University of Aberdeen, where drugs were harder to obtain than in the area surrounding the University of South Florida in the northern suburbs of Tampa. That was where there were lots of subsidized housing and apartments and was known as Suitcase City. It was rife with violent crimes and drug dealers preying on weak individuals.

Nikki and I were also thankful for the quiet time together and rediscovering our relationship—another hidden treasure we were finding there on Little Gasparilla Island.

Our marriage had always been solid to a point for me to know that she would always be there, no matter what. Telling Nikki my feelings that evening felt so good, it was not easy for me to convey my feelings off the cuff or in a casual conversation. I said I would try in the future to be more caring, not because I had to but because deep down, my love was stronger than ever, and I loved being with her. Nikki was very beautiful and smart, with her quickness in conversation at dinner parties or family get-togethers when she would light up the room. It was not only her looks but also her university-schooled, polished English accent that made people stop and listen to what was being said by an attractive five-foot-two blonde with a slim figure. Part of Nikki's signature attire was always wearing her favorite footwear, Birkenstocks, many elegant gold rings, and other beautiful jewelry; she had a special penchant for bracelets and bangles.

Finally, we were ready to walk to the beach. Nikki was in her yellow dress that had a small fish painted on the right side with a pale blue background. Her attire when we went out on the beach, whether we were by ourselves or meeting friends, nearly always had a beach theme. We had a few minutes to go before sunset. Holding hands and with our drinks in the other one, we were just thankful to be there. The sun was magnificent dipping into the water, casting rays through wispy clouds, turning the edges silver. Soon it was time to go home for supper. The only thing we had to do was cut up the chicken; there was no waiting or mess to clean up from the ready-made meal. After eating our simple dinner, we walked Napier one last time before going to bed. Another long, busy day had passed without really being pushed to do anything—ah! I had already gotten the rod and reel ready to use in the morning as I needed to get up early, anyway, to let the dog out. No problem going to sleep, as usual, for all of us.

It seemed like, in no time at all, we were waking up to owls hooting, and it sounded like they were not far away. We both got up and, taking Napier with us, we went to find the owls. They were on top of an Australian pine tree across June's house; we could just make them out in the morning twilight. What a sight! They were the biggest birds both of us had ever seen, horned-ear owls that looked to be almost three feet tall. It was a bonus to see such magnificent creatures. The three of us then went back to have breakfast before walking to the beach and picking up my new fishing pole to cast into the Gulf to see what, if anything, would attack the silver spoon lure. After about a half hour, nothing was biting, probably because it was still a little dark and the lure, even though it looked like a baitfish, didn't have the fishy smell that would have attracted a hungry fish.

Napier soon wanted to head back to the house, where Nikki had returned to earlier to get a little more sleep. I thought we both needed a cup of strong coffee to perk us up. We heard Nikki stirring in the bedroom, and I put the coffeepot on. Napier followed me closely on my way out to the porch. Obviously, she wanted more food or a treat. Nikki staggered out, half asleep, saying, "Coffee, please," as she sat down at the kitchen table, which was also our main table. A light came on next door, which made us think that we had neighbors; as the lady let out her little dog, Napier was raising a ruckus, so Nikki said that I had better go out to deal with it. The lady was in her nightgown, stepping back behind the screen door. After apologizing and at the same time pulling Napier back by her collar, I looked across the lane to see another light that was on, so I decided to go back in with the dog to finish my coffee. I told Nikki that we had two new sets of neighbors.

She said, "I hope they like dogs."

I assured her that the ones next to us have a dog, and that was the reason for all the barking!

After coffee, we all walked to the dock again, hoping Napier would visit the woods and for us to see the sun come up. Two new boats were tied up to the post on different sides of our dock. A man walked up the walkway, with Napier noticing him first, and she barked at the newcomer. We turned around to see a tall, lean man coming toward us with a wondering stare. He stopped for a moment to check out his bowlines, and then he continued to introduce himself as Jerry Ridings.

He asked us, "Where are you folks from?"

We both talked about where we lived permanently, how long we were on the island for, and where we were staying on the lane. He was smitten with Nikki's way of talking and teasingly said with a wide smile, "You don't sound like you are from Georgia."

She replied, "No, Jerry. I'm actually from London, England."

He said, "I don't think I've ever met anyone else who has such an attractive accent."

We enjoyed talking to him; he was such a polite man. But he had to go back for breakfast as Mrs. Ridings had started it when he walked down to check out the boat. We gathered that the second boat belonged to the other new neighbors.

On our way back, we passed the Ridings' house on the right; it had yellow siding and was directly across the lane from June's place. As we arrived back at the house for a cup of tea, the man next door was under his house, getting a golf cart ready to use. We walked over to introduce ourselves. He said that his name was Charlie and mentioned that his wife was upstairs. We went through the whole gamut for several minutes of whom and what we were and found Charlie to be a very pleasant man. Very kindly, he said that if we needed anything, to let them know.

He also told us Mr and Mrs Wallace from across the street had come down from Tampa with them in separate cars. They were going to spend most of the winter there, but Charlie and his wife were staying for the weekend only. Both couples were retired and enjoying life; they were in the fortunate position of being able to have a home in Tampa and a beach house as a bolt-hole.

My main job that day was to climb on the roof to sweep the pine needles off before they could do any damage. Nikki was holding the ladder, and the needles were thick and heavy with moisture from the morning dew. I believed if the job were left undone, rot would set in eventually, and having to do just one domestic job per week wasn't bad at all! Cleaning windows might have to be done next. We were out on the deck admiring the roof when the Wallaces came down the steps, and we introduced ourselves to them. Judy Wallace was very nice, but her husband was not at all social by indicating he did not really want to be bothered meeting someone new. It turned out that Judy and her husband were retired schoolteachers, so they had something in common with Nikki. He walked off while we were telling them that we were there on LGI, hopefully, for at least another ten weeks. I left Nikki and Judy talking to put away the ladder and broom before lunch. Nikki came back to ask if I would help Clare (short for Clarence) Wallace move a chest of drawers, which was in his boat, up the steps to put in their bedroom, so we went down the lane in his golf cart to fetch it back. It was a small chest, thank goodness, and soon the chore was over with. He grunted out a sound that could have been a thank-you.

In the early afternoon, we decided to walk in the middle of the island, southward, after going to the dock first to see if any new boats were moored up. The house on the left or north side, with its own dock, had a fairly large boat tied up close to the shore along their walkway. There was another much larger boat there, with lettering on the back announcing her name as *Peaches*. We then backtracked up the lane a quarter of the way back to the road called Grande Avenue, which went mainly north and south. It was the only way to access the island apart from going by the beach. The lane zigzagged past several private properties because it was a deeded access for everyone's use.

We came across a detached garage with golf carts all around it, and there was a man working on a cart in the front. We stopped to talk to him, and he introduced himself as Bob Pelfrey, and he turned out to be the man to see for purchasing or renting buggies, which was the only form of transport to get around the island.

We continued on Grande Avenue and took a right a hundred yards farther, leading to the Gulf, then headed south again after two hundred yards, going past larger stilt homes facing the Gulf. What great views those places must have had; they were completely different from the houses on Peacock Lane. We had seen loads of animal tracks crossing the lane; most likely, they belonged to turtles. And there were some bobcat-sized tracks too; bobcats were purported to be on the island.

Farther on, where the lane bent left, there was a bordering property where an upscale housing project had started, called the Preserve of LGI. Grande Avenue continued to the left, past sand dunes, then right through the middle of the preserve, with very large lots on the left that were on the Bay; the lots on the right were on the Gulf. We walked onward to find a small white church with a sizable steeple. It was a pleasant discovery. Inside were polished wood pews, and outside, it had parking for a few golf carts!

We had to walk a little farther on to find an access to the beach so that we could walk back to our area looking for sharks' teeth and other treasures. Getting out to the beach, we were very close to the condos called Hideaway Bay Beach Club that had a view of Boca Grande at the southernmost part of LGI. It ended where the little pass separated Gasparilla Island from Little Gasparilla Island. We headed back after walking for more than an hour (if we had gone by beach, we would have been back within half an hour). We felt we could really use a cup of tea and a sit-down.

CHAPTER FIVE

 ## MEETING ISLAND FOLKS

WHILE WE WERE sitting on the front porch, Jerry Ridings walked up to say hello again; he was probably wondering what we were all about. He said, "Ruth is fixing something to eat, which meant it was time to get out of her way or be put to work in the kitchen where I have no business being." Jerry said he knew how to work on cars or trucks in his garage, but working in the kitchen was another story.

We all then started talking about the weather and how "gorgeous" it was, as Nikki described it so well. Not long afterward, a John Deere-type open-top buggy drew up with a large man in it in a brown fishing shirt and a tall much-tanned blond wife beside him. They appeared to look about the same age as us, and they introduced themselves as Ed and Louise Sasser. Ed said in a gruff tone, "What you doing on this island?" And we had to explain ourselves all over again.

Then Nikki said in her posh accent, "Ed, 'what *are* you doing on this island' is the correct way to say it."

We all grinned as Ed also found her remark funny; he had the biggest property on Peacock Lane. It was an imposing-looking tropical estate with many oak trees on the shore of Gasparilla Bay. To add to his man-of-property persona, he was also an orange-grove owner. He always took command and was the boss wherever he was living. Louise, on the other hand, was a very polite Southern lady who told Nikki not to take any notice of him. They had a dog in the back called Snook; we assumed he was named after the local sport fish, which is also a delicious-tasting fish with flaky white meat. The Sassers, like Jerry, were from Wauchula, a small town in the middle of the state in Southwest Florida, approximately two-and-one-half hours from LGI due east with a little jaunt to the north. When we told Ed and Louise that our main home was in Blairsville, Georgia, they told us about a cousin of theirs who was in Hayesville, North Carolina, not far from where we lived. Nikki chimed in with "The first place we lived was a house in Hayesville, up on Cherry Mountain. We rented for the first year to see if the area could support an antique warehouse which would provide merchandise to dealers in the trade."

Ed had asked in his gruff but friendly voice, "Well, did you open your warehouse?"

We assured him that, yes, we did. We rented a warehouse at the bottom of Cherry Mountain on a road that led to Hiawassee and Blairsville. After a year or so, we moved to a large building at Potteet Corner—on the way to Murphy, North Carolina—that once was a gas station and general store in the North Georgia mountains. It was close to Tennessee on Lake Nottely, where lots of summer homes were located, owned by people from Atlanta, only two hours away from the new antique warehouse. We told them that that proved to be the most lucrative move since some summer residents had several vacation homes in Florida or Colorado ski resorts. From the first summer we opened, we sold a lot to tourists stopping by while they were there on vacation or utilizing their summer place, yet we were still supplying dealers from all over the south from Florida to Kentucky to Mississippi. Some dealers would rent a U-Haul from the garage next door to take their purchases back to their respective warehouses in the different states.

While Nikki was telling the story, it brought back many happy thoughts of how fortunate we were that it all worked out. We luckily had been mature enough to handle large amounts of money for purchasing antiques in England and Scotland; we would plow all our takings back into inventory. We'd sometimes gamble and experiment with the little more expensive items that take up less space in a sea freight container, and that allowed us to hopefully sell them for a little more profit. Looking ahead, we still couldn't be frivolous if we were to live comfortably through our retirement years. Nikki was once again telling our life story to new friends!

We had all been out in front of the beach house for quite a while when another couple drove up. They were a little older than us, almost certainly retired, and the man introduced themselves as Dick and Doris Bublitz. He asked Ed in his broad New York twang, "Have you heard from George?"

Ed replied, "He will be in any day now, as early as this weekend. He should be driving down from New Jersey by himself." Ed then suggested that all of us should meet on George's deck for sunset. "I'm sure he would be pleased for us to get his place ready."

Louise said, "Let's all bring something to snack on."

Just after everyone had left, June was walking toward us with her dogs. She said to Nikki, "I see you met most of the neighbors. No doubt they will want to know what you're all about."

Nikki laughed, saying, "I have told our life history so many times in slightly different ways that if they all ever concurred, it would sound like a real concoction of stories!"

She told June that we were all meeting for drinks at five on the deck of the little round house. She added that the Sassers suggested it because we wouldn't be so presumptuous to suggest trespassing on another's property! I then chimed in about going inside to make us a cup of tea before we got ready for the sunset party. While relaxing over a hot cuppa, Nikki couldn't believe how many people had welcomed us to their island. She thought it was marvelous to have so many visits in such a short time. Little did we know that all these new acquaintances would become close friends for years to come? We were both wondering what George Geier was going to be like; everyone seemed to have a "can't wait to see George again for another winter" attitude, not to mention that he had one of the best views of the Gulf from his beach house!

Nikki said, "Lloyd, it is time to get showered, dressed, and prepare our hors d'oeuvres contribution."

I suggested that Nikki get ready first while I fed Napier and took her down to the beach for a walk. About fifteen minutes later, we returned to the house. Nikki looked gorgeous in her beach dress making a tray of nachos with salsa. We were excited about socializing on Peacock Lane that evening.

Ed and Louise were the first to arrive at George's, and we followed close behind to help pull the chairs from the back of the house to an anchored table in front of the deck. As we got it set up, Dick and Doris drove up in their buggy with another couple they introduced as Jesse and Sally, neighbors of the Bublitzes, also with a Bay-front home. June drove up with her dogs, and hors d'oeuvres were brought by everyone. Ed and Louise had a large tray of mullet that he had smoked and frozen some time ago, and they brought saltine crackers to go with the fish. Now there were four dogs—Napier, Snook, Bonnie, and Jasper—and the deck full of local folks. I went back to our house for two more plastic chairs. We were all having different conversations. Jerry walked up to add a thought or two when Ed, after cutting off a chunk to place on a cracker, said to him, "Taste this mullet, Jerry, to see if it measures up to your liking."

Jerry said, "Not bad, Mr. Sasser," and then he blurted out teasingly to everyone, "Now if any of you all want me to translate what this pretty little lady from London says, I'll be glad to."

Ed's comment was simply "Oh brother! I think she has more book-learning than all of us put together."

Jerry was a good guy to have as a friend on the island since he owned a Firestone tire outlet in Wauchula, and he visited the island often, bringing golf cart tires when anyone needed some. June's cart had oversized tires to help deal with the soft sand and had been fitted out by Jerry's company. Ed and Louise's cart, being a wide heavy-duty vehicle, had no problem driving up to George's house where the sand was deep enough to bog down many carts; there were rubber mats trailing into his little detached toolshed that housed his golf cart.

The people at the sunset party were all very enjoyable company, with the guys talking mainly about the fish they had caught or hoped to catch the next day and the women more about other island folk and their homes or their shell collections. We all departed as new friends, our tummies full of smoked mullet, and even the dogs (which were fed morsels of fish) became quickly acquainted.

We went back to our place, which was just a couple of houses down across the lane toward the Bay. On our front porch, we discussed what had gone on at the party with all the different conversations about the people and the island. Nikki said everyone was still as excited as we were to see dolphins feeding in the Gulf and the large number of pelicans diving in for their food; even after living there for many years, it was still a thrill. We could never have imagined being in such an incredible place at that time in our lives. You hear clichés like "Being at the right place at the right time." That was our time to treasure the island. We talked for an hour on the porch then took Napier for her walk before going to bed.

While nodding off to sleep, we both thought the next day would be a good time to unpack the fax machine, other office equipment, as well as the files that had the information we needed for our clients. That would be the start of planning my big trip to Scotland to supply our customers in Florida and Texas. I drifted off to sleep, making plans to go overseas. It always took hours of going over in my mind to make the trip less arduous, like transferring funds into a Royal Bank of Scotland account in Alyth, Scotland, which we had opened twelve years ago. Auction bills had to be paid as soon as I got to the warehouse in Ladybank (about an hour north of Edinburgh by train).

The next morning, I woke up again in paradise at the same time as Nikki; she wanted to call the children in Britain before setting up the fax, just in case I somehow screwed up the wiring! We talked a while before getting up to let the dog out as Napier was still sleepy, and then I got up to make our morning coffee. We both planned and replanned my trip. That day would still give us the best rate for an airline ticket with a two-week advance fare; there was a lot to do for both of us.

Nikki called our daughter, Julliet, to say that I hoped to visit her when heading back to London. Then she called Jonathan and told him we were counting on him to help load containers the weekend he'd be out of school. That would provide me with a much-needed hand loading heavy furniture and would pay back some of the funds we had allocated to him every month.

After calling the kids, Nikki talked to her friends Jimetta in Tampa and Ro in Canada and then said to me, "The phone is now yours. You better call the airlines for a quote for two weeks today or tomorrow, whichever will be cheaper."

I was planning a two-week trip, hoping to come back quicker if the work went quickly and smoothly. She also suggested that I call my clients first to see when they would like their shipments to arrive. Nikki was right; maybe their business will dictate when they would want another container packed.

After calling our client John Benton in Tampa, he said he was about to call me in Georgia, which surprised me as I thought we had let everyone know where we were going to be that winter. He stated that he would like the container of antiques to arrive a few days before January the first so that he could plan a New Year's Day sale.

Now I had to call the Austin, Texas, auction house. Ross, the owner, answered the phone, saying he also was thinking about calling me. He wanted to have a big auction on New Year's Day, usually a lucrative beginning to the year. Next, I had to call Delta or British Air for the best price from Sarasota to London through Atlanta. After talking to both the airlines, Delta was the best price: leaving on a Monday from Sarasota at noon and arriving in London on Tuesday morning around 6:00 a.m. Then I would take the train up to Scotland. So that job was done.

Now, finally, it was time to set up the fax for John and Ross so that they could fax me a wish list as guidance of what to buy for them. Nikki and I took Napier to the beach to discuss what she thought regarding things I should do and whom I should visit while in England. She said she was going to miss me dreadfully, and I certainly didn't want to think about missing her. June was on the phone a few hours later to tell Nikki that if she needed to go to the mainland while I was gone, she would gladly take her in her boat.

My trip was planned for two weeks, but I really hoped to cut it short if I could get everything done. I started to put things in my old leather suitcase as the days went by. First thing to go in would be my insulated boots and long wool socks, which were very important, as were my work gloves and a heavy sweater. Something that must not be forgotten was the large sandwich that Winn-Dixie made out of one of their Italian loaves filled with all types of meat and cheese called the manhandler. That sandwich would last me the nine-hour train ride from Gatwick Airport to Ladybank Station in Scotland.

There was lots of packing and repacking over the next two weeks, checking with Julliet about what the weather was likely to be, but at that moment, it was to get back to the beach house for a much-needed cup of tea. While we were on the porch, the fax was receiving a message, probably from one of our clients. It was a list from John with specific orders to fill half a container with two-, three-, and four-door wardrobes that could be kitted out as entertainment centers and as many cocktail cabinets and sideboards as I could get, along with the usual number of pub tables. I told Nikki that I might have to go by Pierre's warehouse in Walsall for a number of French armoires if Jimmy didn't have any in stock or any coming up for auction soon. (He owned the Ladybank auction house. I'd let him know what I wanted, and he would buy for me.)

I put a list in the suitcase so as not to misplace it. Nikki suggested that I make an extra copy to stay with her just in case the luggage went missing, and I could call her to get the information. Thinking about what was needed to put in the case for Scotland would go on for days; I could not forget the Scottish checkbook or my address book (after calling necessary people and banks as early as the next day). Transferring funds in plenty of time is essential to make sure the money is there before leaving the States so that Jimmy could be paid in full before leaving Ladybank. These plans and thoughts were swirling through my mind, but no more for that day; I needed to spend time with Nikki and Napier.

We got back on the subject of the party the day before; we did enjoy meeting all the new people at sunset. Nikki thought that it was probably going to be a common occurrence for the rest of the winter. We took our bucket to collect shells. Just to be together wading in the water with the dog was wonderful; we found the water cool at first, and then, after a short time, it felt fine splashing along, with the dog running in the shallows. Nikki read for the rest of the afternoon. We didn't really have a proper lunch, just helped ourselves to snacks, and I had a late nap along with Napier. As she was wet, she had to sleep out on the porch with Nikki by the swing. After my nap, the dog and I walked to the dock with a fishing rod.

The Sassers were on the porch, giving us a wave as we walked by. Ed walked over while I kept the lure moving in the water, asking what I was trying to catch. I responded with "Anything, Ed," hoping it was something that we could have for supper. I told him that the smoked mullet we had the day before at sunset had been a treat and that it had been years since we'd had it.

He said, "Come over, and I'll give you enough for supper tonight."

I followed him over to his porch that had a most wonderful view of the Bay. Louise asked if I'd like a glass of iced tea.

"Sure would," I replied.

Napier came onto the porch with me, but Snook wasn't so sure that was a good idea. She gave Napier a slight growl.

"Oh, hush," Ed said to his dog.

They were country folk from Florida, or Florida Crackers, as most of my relatives are, along with me. We kind of got along without saying it. After almost an hour, Nikki came looking for us. Louise said for her to come up, and we visited for another half hour before saying that we had to get back to get ready for sunset and supper. They gave me the smoked mullet, and off we went. Nikki said she had been worried about us since we were gone so long.

After sunset and supper, we settled down for the night, wondering what the next day was going to bring. The next couple of days were full of shelling and reading for Nikki and fishing for me, but with no fish to show for my efforts. Maybe some shrimp for bait would change my luck. That spoon lure just wasn't getting the job done.

The next day was the day to contact Jimmy in Scotland, the bank in Georgia to transfer funds, and the taxi company in Englewood—but firstly, to call John and Ross to see if their funds

LLOYD ARTHUR WIGGINS AND ROSEMARY EGERTON LETTS

had been wired to my bank. The fax from Ross came in; his funds, along with John's, were in my account. Our Georgia bank had now sent the money through Wachovia and, eventually, to their office in London. The funds would be in my account at the Royal Bank of Scotland in Alyth within three days.

Then it was time to speak to Jimmy, who lived in a beautiful rural setting next to the warehouse on the edge of a forest. His house was surrounded by trees with no other houses in sight; he and his wife Maureen had a kit house built, which was exported from Canada and resembled a stone cottage. It was a well-insulated two-story house that, in Scotland, was rare because most of the homes were made of local stone (mostly granite) that was cold year round.

Getting through to Jimmy, he said he had everything ready for my arrival: plenty of gear, packing materials, blankets, and twenty rolls of six-foot-tall corrugated paper for wrapping furniture. The wool blankets were picked up and saved from house clearances and used for packing finished or highly polished furniture. The first container ordered from Barton Freight Services was to arrive the morning after I got there.

When I had everything set up in the UK, I was going to call a taxi company in Englewood when Nikki suggested that I not take a taxi but drive our car to the long-term parking at the airport so that when I got back, it would be there waiting for me, and it would only be an hour's drive or less to Eldred's. Nikki said that she couldn't see herself leaving the island unless it was with June, and she could then go in her car to the grocery store or into town.

Nikki then called the Bevans to tell them that I'd be in England in two weeks' time and that I hoped to see them on the way back to Gatwick in about three and a half weeks. She was on the phone to Jacque for at least thirty minutes, mainly talking about the children—having four between us, all in their early twenties—there were lots to talk about.

After coming off the phone, Nikki said the Bevans were looking forward to me dropping by and said I could stay as long as I would like to. Nikki asked if there was anyone else that I wanted to visit, and I said that, of course, I would like to see Julliet in Newcastle and to have Jonathan join me at the warehouse. I would also like to visit the Claytons near Gatwick Airport, but not to stay with them because I would have reservations at the travel lodge across from Gatwick's north terminal. I was hoping to meet up with a Barton Freight representative for dinner that night at the hotel. I told her that I was sure we were forgetting something or someone.

I would wear my pinstripe wool suit just in case the airline needed to upgrade a frequent flyer, and it would keep me warm during the train trip up north to Scotland. British Rail's heating didn't work and was sometimes not even turned on; it had been very cold on some of the trains in the past. I was getting a little excited about going and, at the same time, feeling a little mournful at the thought of leaving Nikki and Napier for a couple of weeks; I guess it was really a case of mixed emotions. We all have to do things to make a living, and I was so grateful to be doing what I did and being my own boss.

The day was coming to a close. There was no sunset that evening as there was too much cloud cover; it looked like maybe a front was coming in. Early to bed meant getting a good start the next day.

Waking up at the crack of dawn, with Nikki and Napier still asleep, was a good time to have a cup of coffee while again trying to think of stuff that had to be done for my trip. The first thing was to find my passport, my British driver's license, and my British Rail card, along with the currency left over from the last trip—coins for the phone box to let friends and children know where I was in London or at the airport, waiting for a train to catch. If the train connections were too close, I could use the pay phone on the train; they are a little noisy, but I guess it adds to the atmosphere.

Napier came out to the porch asking for her breakfast, and I heard Nikki making enquiries about coffee from the bedroom. After I completed my list, we just lounged the rest of the morning away.

Nikki finally called Cynthia to see how the sales had been going for the last couple of weeks. She told Nikki that the weather was not bad, which brought people up to the lake to winterize their summer homes, and they would stop by to find things for Christmas to give as presents or use for decorating, so sales were good. Nikki helped me finalize the itinerary for Scotland and England.

George getting to know Napier

Going for Water

John and his Thoughts

Fileting fish

Trolling

Going Home

Loading up

On the intercoastal

going out for lunch

the elusive birds

Nikki with her Aunt Philly

June's boat

Catch of the day with Ed Strickland

CHAPTER SIX

 GEORGE

NIKKI, NAPIER, AND I strolled down to the dock to see if the mullet were jumping and watch ospreys diving into Gasparilla Bay. While we were sitting on the dock, a boat came in with a smiling, handsome, older-looking man who was maybe in his late seventies, driving a somewhat vintage boat. We found out later that he was, in fact, eighty-three. At the dock, there was a vintage golf cart backed up to the side of the walkway. Everything was starting to fit; someone had brought George's cart down, knowing that he was going to arrive sometime that day.

He shouted for us to tie his boat up to the front left piling so he could reverse sideways into the dock by using the taut line to swing his boat around. He then threw the other ropes out for us to tie the boat up close so that he could unload his gear. Before handing his cargo out, the man stuck out his hand to introduce himself as George Geier. Nikki and I responded in a likewise manner. He passed out suitcases, boxes of provisions, jugs of water, plus other odds and ends. He got out of his boat to retie his lines while we loaded up his cart. Nikki got in his cart to ride up with him, as did Napier, sitting on the floor, for George to ask, "Who invited him?"

Nikki said, "*Him* is a *her*."

We both noticed how piercingly blue his eyes were, and he seemed to have a teasing way about him. I followed behind, trying to walk as fast as possible, which wasn't really necessary as we had to wait for him to open up his house. We started to off-load his buggy onto the deck. He had to clear up inside with newspapers on his floor and kitchen table, as insect foggers had been let off just before his departure.

Now George was slowly getting his home opened up for the winter. He turned on the electrics so the air conditioner could help air out the musty smell. Then, with crossed fingers, he said, "Let's hope the water pump starts up."

After everything was in the house, George thanked us for stacking all his gear inside for him to put away and then asked us to join him on his deck at sunset for cocktails, and he added, "Don't bring anything because the Geier Seaside Lounge will be officially open for business."

Nikki replied with a thank-you and said that we would see him at five. She asked, "Could we bring Napier?"

And he replied, "I don't know who that is."

Nikki said, "You gave her a ride up to your house from the dock."

Chuckling, he said, "Sure, if she could handle her drink without going on all fours or barking at the moon."

As we were leaving, Dick pulled up just before Ed and Louise arrived to welcome George back to his little red round house on the shore. We walked back across the road to our place to the sounds of "Nice to see you again, George" and lots of friendly chitchat.

We had just over an hour to shower, feed the dog, and get our meal ready for later. Nikki thought it might be polite to give George extra time to unpack and get ready to entertain. She said, "Lloyd, some of his two-and-a-half-gallon water jugs were really heavy. George couldn't possibly carry them inside."

When we looked over, they weren't on the deck, so someone else must've helped him, probably Ed or Dick. A little later on, we kept looking over to see if he was going to come out on the deck. He did at around five thirty, looking to see if we were on our way, so then we walked over. I took my drink with me and left George to fix Nikki's, as he had suggested. He probably wouldn't have my favorite brand of red wine. Walking up his ramp with Napier glancing over at him, George said, "You're late."

Nikki replied "Politely late, George!" in her very English accent. "A socially acceptable courtesy, just in case the host was running late."

George replied, "A nice way of saying it, instead of 'sorry, I'm late.'"

Nikki also laughed, saying, "Touché, George."

That broke the ice, and we both felt we could be ourselves without having to watch what we said. You never know what to expect when socializing with new people for the first time; getting acquainted with a cautious, polite behavior was a must as we were all to be neighbors for a few months. We were made to feel very comfortable.

Settling down in large plastic armchairs, George was about to give us a history lesson on the last three decades of the immediate area. We couldn't wait to learn as much as possible and catch up on more information about that beautiful part of Florida.

George pointed to an iron pipe sticking out of the sand by about a foot. He said that that was a casing for a house that used to be in front of his house close to twenty years ago. Thirty years ago, there was another house in front of that one. When he bought his place, there were two houses in front of him, and now he was beachfront. The two houses on the left, with pilings in the surf, would surely be next to go. George then talked about his beautiful late wife, Ingrid, who was his rock for over fifty years and who had died not long ago and of their lives when they were young when George worked on the docks, alongside unions rife with organized crime. He was an entrepreneur in his day, recycling burlap sacks from various ships along with other endeavors on the waterfront. He told us of having a nickname given to him by the head mafia boss Anastasia: "Georgie the Bags." George founded Agmarine Contracting Company, a marine maintenance company in Brooklyn, New York, in the 1940s, later expanding his company to New Orleans. He also went over his earlier times as a bartender on Miami Beach and how he loved to show off his talent mixing cocktails.

George went to fix another scotch and soda for Nikki as I excused myself to go back home to get another Cabernet on ice, cut with an ounce of water. George said, "Next time, I will have your favorite wine here after I've gone shopping." He sat down again and asked, "How long are you here for?"

We replied, "Another two or three months or when the last of our guests from the United Kingdom leave."

George got up from the table to fix more drinks and then brought out a plate of sliced sausages with sesame seed crackers to snack on. Nikki said, "George, we have some snacks in the house to add to yours."

He said, "No, I told you not to bring anything tonight, but I understand Lloyd bringing his drink as I didn't have his brand of choice."

He started to tell us about the cost of salt erosion on appliances and outside equipment and how he had needed to buy a new engine for his boat last year; the cost was about twelve thousand dollars. I told George that it really didn't look that new to me; in fact, it was the first thing I noticed, that someone had spray-painted it an awful color trying to cover up the original, and it looked terrible. He laughed to say that was the purpose, to deter someone from stealing it since, not too long ago, a son of a resident had stolen a couple of engines to sell on the mainland.

As we sat there, we saw a dolphin leap out of the water with a young one tucked to her side; it was a wonderful sight, and we could tell George was glad to be back on LGI again. He sat way back in his chair, enjoying the warm breeze and the salty smell while watching the sun setting into the water. We all sat there quietly for a few moments, not needing to talk, just taking in the beauty of it all.

After saying good night, George commented on Napier being a very well-behaved dog—she was good for once, especially with food close by, which was rare. I mentioned we had to walk Napier down the lane before it got too dark, and pretty soon, we were back to our dinner with a cup of coffee on the porch before turning in for the night. In bed, we sat up, anticipating what the next day would bring.

I said to Nikki, "Darling, I do love you so much and love being with you."

After a good night's sleep, Napier touched my hand early in the morning with her cold nose to say she needed to go out. "Okay, okay," I said, with Nikki whispering to me to put the coffee on please, as she promised to fix breakfast in a few minutes. After letting Napier out and putting the coffee on, I glanced over at George's to see if there were lights on or any activity; he was most likely tired from his long drive south.

Nikki was up getting our toast ready. She wanted to go looking for sharks' teeth, a new treasure to search for while collecting shells. After an hour of walking, talking, and looking for treasures on the beach, it was time to go back for another coffee. Walking by George's house, there was still no sign of activity. That could be a good thing, for he must have been getting some rest. The way he moved concerned me; he seemed to shuffle rather than walk. That was probably why someone had his cart ready at the dock because he was not able to walk all the way to his house from his boat.

"We could certainly help him if he needs us," Nikki commented. Then she wanted to talk and plan about me leaving soon and go over last-minute details. She said, "At least, we will have this weekend to mentally get ready to be apart for two weeks," hoping it would be less. "I think Napier and I both will feel like something is wrong when you're not here, Lloyd."

I told Nikki that every time I commute to England, my feeling of loneliness would be overwhelming. When the plane takes off, I think of her while I try to sleep on the long flight from Atlanta to London. Then when I take the Thameslink train from Gatwick, a ninety-minute ride to London's King's Cross Station, to catch the Edinburgh Flying Scotsman train that left at 9:00 a.m., I would still be thinking of her. Once I was on it, I'd be pretty well exhausted, and sleep came easy. My missing her would only invade my inner self again when I settled down to sleep in the warehouse.

I had been through this commuting now for almost four years; I still felt the same way on leaving. When the job was over, the feeling was opposite; I would be excited to be returning to Nikki and America. When I passed over Newfoundland, looking out the airplane window, a euphoric feeling would overwhelm me, a wonderful feeling inside of being over North America. I knew this trip would be the same; I hoped to be calling Nikki from a phone box whenever I could in the UK, often on train platforms while waiting for the next train to wherever I was going.

Everything had been worked out. No need to dwell on the trip until Monday. We looked forward to seeing George at five o'clock for sunset, then who knows what the weekend would bring?

A short lie-down was needed while listening to the waves while I still mulled over in my mind about me leaving in a few days. I could not help thinking that I should go to the mainland to shop so that Nikki wouldn't have to go over on a boat. I also remembered that I must call Julliet and Jonathan that Saturday to let them know that I hoped to see them in the next week or two.

After a thirty-minute nap, we took the dog for a walk to the dock. When passing June's house, we spoke to her out in her side garden to let her know we would be on George's dock at sunset. She said that she would mosey on down after five. We got to the end of the lane and sat on the Bay. It was blissfully quiet, with the sound of fish jumping. We stayed for twenty minutes or so, taking in the scene, then Nikki suggested we should go back, for it was time to shower and get the snacks ready.

The shower water hadn't improved; Nikki said it was still awfully brown and smelly, and she did not like washing her hair in it. That was one continuous subject that would probably never change! Also, we were always asking each other where the time went. And even what day it was. Time seemed to fly by even with no papers or television, just a radio for news.

The next day was Friday, and I would need to go to Englewood for water, food, and a *Tampa Tribune* plus a local paper. I also had to get something other than potato chips or salsa to take to George's, as well as stock up with supplies. Nikki said we should make a list in the morning, but right then, we needed to feed the dog before going across the road for sunset. I hoped George didn't mind us inviting June over to join us on his deck. After another five minutes, George was already sitting out in his chair, waiting for us. When we told George that June was coming for sunset, he said that it would be fine; in fact, the more the merrier. Just as we were speaking about her, we could see June driving her cart up the lane toward us with her two dogs.

When we all settled down in our deck chairs, Nikki told everyone that I was leaving Monday for London to go and earn some pennies; they thought that it was a little extreme to have to commute that far. She said, "We both go together sometimes, when the need arises, but Lloyd has to go by himself about six times a year."

We were enjoying a very pleasant evening watching the Gulf, again hoping to see the green flash that happens only occasionally just as the sun goes down—quite an amazing sight! George was making the drinks for himself and Nikki. June brought her favorite gin with tonic with a twist of lime while I was sipping my red wine, just to be sociable. Laughingly, no one believed that was the real reason.

While gazing out to sea, fish were seen about two hundred yards offshore. George thought they could be Spanish mackerel migrating south, chasing baitfish. Birds were feeding on them, and the dolphins were eating too. It was most likely mackerel. With all the activity in the water, George asked if I would like to go fishing the following morning. He said he would call Dick to meet us on our dock about ten.

I said, "Sure. Is there anything for me to do to help you get ready?"

He said the rod and reels were already set up for trolling for mackerel. "Just bring water or whatever you needed to drink."

Getting ready to go to our house, we all agreed it was another beautiful sunset, but no green flash that time. After all of us said our good-byes, we headed back down the lane. Nikki decided to walk with June and her dogs toward her house in the dark to give Napier a little exercise. The weekend would soon be over, and time was closing in fast to catch that plane Monday morning. The packing was finally done.

I woke up Saturday morning full of expectation about the fishing trip that day, and I needed to call the Florida Game and Fish Commission to buy a license over the phone. It was the first time I'd done it that way instead of going to a bait shop or Walmart. There was no problem acquiring the license; they told me to just jot down the license number for immediate use and to show my driver's license for an ID while the real license would be mailed within days.

George picked me up on the way to the dock with all the kit in the back of his cart; Dick was already there, waiting for us. After going through the small pass into the Gulf for approximately a mile, George said, "Look for birds feeding on baitfish."

We spotted a lot of them to our left, a little farther out. Getting closer, Dick and I let the line out to use for trolling. The silver spoon lures were doing the trick, and it was only minutes before we were catching good-sized mackerel. In an hour, we caught ten fish, enough for a feast that night. Then it was back to the dock to fillet our catch.

On the ride back to our dock through the Little Gasparilla Pass, we saw people collecting shells on the south end of the island, very close to the waterway where our wake was washing ashore onto a small piece of land some locals call Shell Island. When we got back, George took control of the filleting, and I could see why: he was a master at saving as much meat as possible. Growing up, we always scaled our fish and fried everything except the innards; filleting was much quicker and not as messy. After finishing the chore, we all agreed to be at George's for a fry-up that evening.

George dropped me off at my house and said, "See you on my deck at five." Spotting Nikki on the porch, he spoke loudly for us to make baked beans or fries to go with the fish.

With an okay back to George, she was pleased to hear we caught enough fish to feed us all. Nikki said, "You smell like a fisherman, so go and have a shower before I make you a cup of tea and a sandwich, then you can have a nap before walking the dog."

While having lunch, I told her all about our fishing escapades and how George drove the boat, trolling at about four miles an hour, while Dick and I alternated pulling in the mackerel. I told her that trolling was a lot more enjoyable than dangling a line over the edge of a boat; you just sat in a chair until the planer brought the fish to the top of the water. Both of those guys knew more about fishing than I probably would ever learn.

During my rest, Nikki was cooking baked beans with barbecue sauce mixed in and smoky bacon covering the top. The wonderful aroma permeating through the house got my and Napier's attention. She said we would leave the baked beans in the oven to stay warm while we went on our walk.

Soon it was time to get ready for the fish fry party. Shortly after five, George came out onto his deck, saw us on our porch, and motioned for us to come over. That would give him a few minutes to socialize with us before starting to fry the fish. He asked what we were doing the next day, which was Sunday.

Nikki replied, "When you all were fishing, I read a notice on a telephone pole while walking to the library, of a service being held in the little white church on the island at eleven in the morning, and we would like to attend. After that, Lloyd and I will have a quiet afternoon, getting ready for him to go to work on Monday."

Dick and Doris were just pulling in, carrying a covered dish for the fish supper, when Nikki blurted out, "Oh my, I left the beans in the oven!"

She hurried over to see how they were, and George said, "I kind of like my baked beans with a little bit of crusty caramel on top."

She was back in a jiffy, relieved that they had been left on a low temperature. By now, George and Nikki were frying fish, leaving me to set the table on the deck. Dick was taking care of Doris, who was feeling poorly but looking as elegant as a New York executive would be expected to look. Everyone was now at the table, and we were ready to enjoy the day's catch. The food was superbly prepared, and there was plenty of it, with leftovers for everyone to take a plate home.

We all departed, with George saying to me, "I will gladly take you over to the marina, where your car is, in the morning."

I said, "Thank you very much, George, for a wonderful evening, and I'll see you tomorrow."

CHAPTER SEVEN

 THE LONG COMMUTE TO SCOTLAND

AS HE HAD promised, George gave me a lift to Eldred's Marina where I picked up the car to drive to Sarasota to catch the Delta flight to Atlanta, connecting with the five thirty flight to London, Gatwick. Just thinking about being away for two weeks made me miss being with Nikki on the island already!

It was easy parking at the long-term lot at the airport, and it was just a short walk up to the terminal. Thankfully, the ticket counter was not busy. A Delta employee in a suit walked out of the back area that I recognized as a fellow workmate at Tampa Airport, when I worked for Delta in the seventies.

Dixon said, "What are you doing flying out of here?"

He was the station manager, and I told him all about the little island south where my wife and I were spending the winter. He said he was very pleased to see me, and it seemed that both of us were doing well.

Connections went well in Atlanta, with me getting to the gate in time to preboard the jumbo jet aircraft where I settled in for a nine-hour flight, having been upgraded to business class; it was very nice to have enough room to scrunch up in an extrawide L-1011 leather chair. The seats were larger and reclined quite a bit further than in economy.

I dined and slept my way across the Atlantic very pleasantly, arriving in Gatwick with just a small carry-on for a quick getaway. After going through British immigration, I made my way to the rail station inside the airport for the eight-hour ride to Ladybank, about one hour north of Edinburgh. Sleeping a lot and reading the *Daily Telegraph* newspaper helped pass the time away. After a journey of approximately nineteen hours since leaving dock 88, I arrived at Ladybank Train Station, a building similar to the ones you see in the movies from the Victorian era or World War II. With my case in hand, I walked the fifteen minutes to the warehouse that was to be my home for the next two weeks. I was very fortunate that it wasn't raining, only gloomy and cold.

Jimmy Johnson was waiting in the warehouse since he knew how long my journey would take after calling him from Edinburgh to let him know I had arrived in Scotland. He asked if it was okay to go through the paperwork right away so that we could see where we both stood, while settling my account that had been outstanding for two months. We discussed the pricing and how much more volume was needed for loading at least two forty-foot-high cube containers. It was good to be busy, which helped me stay awake as long as possible, which would help with the jet lag and the five-hour time difference. Drinking several cups of good strong tea was also a nice antidote to stay somewhat alert.

Since Jimmy and Maureen lived next door to where I was packing the container, it was convenient for us to work together on getting things done. After having his supper, Jimmy came over again with his two Doberman pinschers about 8:00 p.m. to see how the cataloging was going and went on to walk the dogs. When he got back, he invited me over for coffee and cake. I told Jimmy it was a relief to be in a warm home after the freezing warehouse, where one could hang meat without it going off. Maureen said for me to be careful that night because the temperature would drop to the low teens. After about forty-five minutes in their comfortable house, it was getting harder and harder to keep my eyes open. They encouraged me to call Nikki before going to bed so that she wouldn't be worrying about me. I made a quick phone call to let her know I'd arrived, and she said to tell Jimmy and Maureen hi and that she and Napier were missing me terribly. She said that the weather was balmy and breezy on the island—such a contrast to where I was. After we both said our good-byes, it was time to get back to the warehouse and my bedroom and office combined. Jimmy said I should put the electric fire on so that he wouldn't find a frozen corpse in the morning! I said good night to Maureen, Jimmy, and the Dobermans, who were very laid back and friendly but did look ferocious.

I got into bed with the fire on, but before long, I had to get up to turn it off when it was getting a little too warm. Daydreaming of Nikki and the island helped me fall asleep quickly; however, I woke up two hours later freezing cold—there seemed to be ice on my mustache! After turning the electric heaters on for about twenty minutes, I had to get out of bed to see what had tripped the security lights outside. It was probably just a rabbit. Then turning the heater off, I went back to sleep quickly. Approximately three hours later, I woke up freezing cold yet again. There had been a hard frost during the night, and it looked like snow outside the window.

After turning the heater back on and making a cup of coffee to go with a couple of pieces of toast, it was then time to brave the freezing warehouse and finish off the manifest for the Florida container. That one was going to be the easiest because John always wanted at least twenty-five armoires and twenty-two buffets, filled in with chests of drawers, tables, lots of oak chairs, and all the cocktail cabinets that could be found. The volume of large furniture made easy work of quickly filling the container.

John's container had to be finished by Saturday afternoon and was to be picked up later that same day. Thursday came; it was another cold, frosty night waiting for delivery from the Ladybank auction house (Jimmy was the owner/auctioneer) by Doogie and Janice, who do most of Ladybank's auction deliveries. They showed up two hours late, which was typical and slightly annoying. After saying our hellos, we off-loaded his truck into the yard where the Florida container was being loaded. There were little camping caravans parked close to the container as Jimmy rented space to the caravan owners. I was in the container packing; Doogie and Janice were sitting on the back of their van, waiting for me to pick out a piece of furniture that would fit into a tight space.

The wind got up and blew a cheap plywood wardrobe into a smart-looking caravan, just missing the window but gouging a hole beneath it! Jimmy let out a loud yell while jumping straight up in the air and seemed to do a three-hundred-degree pirouette, saying, "That ten-quid piece of junk that no one would ever want has damaged my bank manager's brand-new caravan!"

I had to hide behind a large wardrobe in hysterics at seeing Jimmy's seething red face up in the air. Oh god, tears of laughter were streaming down my face. Despite being rather short and somewhat stocky, Jimmy could perform such an acrobatic move, probably because he was a black belt in judo. He was so upset he had to leave for a while, and Doogie was in trouble because he was the scapegoat. Doogie and Janice crept away soon after.

A couple of hours later, Jimmy returned, still beside himself—upsetting one's bank manager is no small thing. I just listened, biting my tongue, giving no opinion. He said he would angle the caravan so his bank manager couldn't spot the damage right away. Another plan Jimmy had in mind was to be around to help him hitch the caravan up to his car and always be in a position so that his own back would cover up the damage. Oh my, how I would laugh, when he wasn't around to see me, at the thought of the whole episode.

Jimmy took me over to preview the weekly Friday auction on Thursday night so that my bids could be left. There were a few pieces that I thought were really nice; I would have to allow a bit more room so they could be loaded early Saturday, to finish off John's container.

Saturday morning arrived, with Jimmy coming over with the breakdown of what was bought for me at the auction. He said it was easily a truckful, with Doogie promising to deliver the furniture by 10:00 a.m. Jimmy and his helper loaded everything outside the auction room, and we waited for Doogie, but there was still no Doogie by noon. It started to snow; the container changeover was a few hours away at 4:00 p.m., when it would start getting dark. The paperwork had to be completed and the door sealed before the container left.

Jimmy came to the warehouse to get me at two o'clock so we could hastily load his truck in order to unload it as needed to put into the container. He was saying that he was going to kill Doogie, who had gone to a wedding with a ceilidh afterward without telling anyone of his change of plans. We got back to the warehouse where the furniture from the auction had to be staged outside to manifest and label before loading. After twenty minutes, there were two inches of snow on the tops of the furniture; I brushed it off to get it into the container when Jimmy said, "Lloyd, you're on your own, I have a wedding to be at in less than an hour."

What a day! The container changeover should still be okay if the pieces fitted together as well as I had planned.

The new container arrived early, and it was going to take another few hours for me to load it on my own. The driver was very nice as he handed me the pieces that were needed to finish the job. He fudged the time so that there would be no penalty for me not having it ready. I gave him a twenty-pound note as a tip, and he was on his way, a little richer after a ninety-minute delay.

It was my mistake; I had got the time wrong, according to my paperwork from Barton Freight Services. Oh well, all's well that ends well.

It was still early in the evening when I walked back to Ladybank in the snow for my supper of fish and chips, eating it on the way back to the warehouse. I must say they were some of the best fish and chips I'd ever had, wrapped in old newspaper, with a good soaking of vinegar and ketchup. I washed the grease off my hands before turning in with my tummy full; there was enough time for a light cocktail, then it was off to sleep.

On Sunday morning, I woke up early again even though the security lights came on during the night, waking me up several times. A rabbit or some other varmint was tripping them. Nights were usually very dark with no streetlights, so when the security lights came on, they tended to wake me up. That early morning, the snow on the ground made it a little lighter to see. I worked all day, starting with the manifests and then labeling items that had to be loaded the following Monday morning. There was now enough room in the large warehouse to line up furniture ready to take out to the loading area for the next container to be loaded. That would help me fill the next shipment a little faster. Hooray! I could possibly set off early to either visit family or friends or go back to the island sooner than planned.

Jimmy came over to the warehouse with his two dogs before walking them in the forest that bordered his buildings. He told me that there was a man who lived in the village who was looking for casual work at seven pounds an hour if I needed any help loading. Jimmy reminded me that that young man had actually worked for me sometime in the past to set up an auction. I agreed, provided he could handle the heavy and awkward furniture, and Jimmy, with a deep breath, said, "Aye, he has a strong back. You needn't worry about our Derek."

I said, "Great, we could probably knock this baby out in a few days."

I was hoping my son Jonathan, who was attending Aberdeen University at the time, would have helped that weekend. After calling him, he said he would try to make it down, but knowing that he would rather party than work, I was pretty sure he wouldn't show. That's life; you have to make the best with what is given to you. That night, Jimmy and Maureen asked me over for supper with a wee dram of whiskey before a delicious meal of meat pie with peas, potatoes, and gravy. Maureen was a very good cook as one could tell by Jimmy's build: he was not fat, but he was not lean either. I said good night to them and thanked them for a home-cooked meal, which was so appreciated and especially nice on a Sunday.

It was a very cold and frosty night, which usually meant a sunny day to follow. I woke up when the security lights came on, which was good since the electric heater needed to be turned on for fifteen minutes. I then got up to get busy with the paperwork and then on to loading the Tampa container. It always seemed a good combination, coffee and paperwork. I had to call Barton Freight Services with the totals. I always liked to speak to Tony, the owner, if I could, but Monday-morning calls were normally busy, and you never knew whom you were going to get, so of course I got one of his helpers, which worked out okay. There was still another hour before Derek was to show up for a long, hard day of work.

Derek walked into the warehouse, and I remembered him from the past ten years, hanging around the auction house. He introduced himself and said he was ready to get stuck in, and we both worked well together. After nine hours, the container was half loaded; Derek asked if he could be paid for the day since the bairns (babies) needed food. He told me he had eight children by two different wives and had been on the dole (unemployment rolls) for a dozen years. He said he couldn't find a real job that would pay him equal to his benefits of three hundred pounds a week since he had no qualifications or enough schooling. I gave him his money, and off he went, whistling down the road.

I made some toast for my supper along with a bowl of canned soup and then had to start labeling and cataloging for Tuesday. At that rate, I would be finished a few days ahead of time, so maybe I could visit Julliet in Newcastle where she attended university. Also, for one night, I hoped to visit our old friends, Jackie and David Bevan, in Hathersage before flying out of Gatwick on the following Saturday morning.

Tuesday morning, there was again a heavy frost, so maybe there would be another sunny day. I started moving furniture in a long row to go out the door to be loaded on the container. I then called Tony at Barton to have them picked up on Wednesday at noon. I called Julliet to see if she had room for me Wednesday night, and she said, "Yes, it will be great to see you, Dad!" Then I called Jackie and David to see if I could stop by Thursday night; they said that they too were looking forward to seeing me. Jackie grew up with Nikki in Harrow, on the outskirts of London, so we all go back to the 1960s.

Derek was on time, and we started off with a bang since it was sunny and had been amazingly dry for two straight days. The sun resting on the container made it hot enough to have just a shirt on with no sweater. Derek asked why anyone would want to go to Spain, because you couldn't beat that Scottish weather. I sort of let it slip by as I did not want a debate on the British climate. Again, after paying off my helper, he went whistling down the road, saying he might drop by the pub before heading home.

Five o'clock came quickly as I settled joyfully down with the paperwork along with a large scotch and water, celebrating all the week's work done. Jimmy came over with the dogs and asked me if I wanted to walk in the forest, and I said that it would be a treat. Even though a little tired, I was euphoric about going back to LGI to be with Nikki next Saturday.

While walking the dogs, Jimmy and I talked about our businesses and how wonderful it was to be working for ourselves. It was now time to go back to the warehouse to finish up last-minute additions to the manifest. I went to bed early after washing my face, hands, and arms and applying hand lotion to help soothe the cracked skin on my palms and fingers. That night, it was not as cold as previously, and it even looked like it might snow.

I had to leave as early as possible in the morning, so I called Barton to give them the final totals, and Jimmy came over to say that the weather forecast was not looking too good. I told him that last night, it looked like it could snow, but thank God it had held off so far. I asked him if he could make sure that the container got away at noon so I might possibly be in front of the band of bad weather, and he said he would be glad to. My bags were packed; the dirty linens were piled on the bed.

I was ready to walk to Ladybank Station when Jimmy said, "Lloyd, you haven't shaved or showered in over a week, and with your old, rough leather suitcase, the police will think you have been dossing out."

I told Jimmy that Edinburgh Train Station had a large area for showering and shaving, and a towel only cost a pound. I would be as right as rain if they didn't throw me off the train before getting to Waverly Station.

I got on the train at Ladybank Station, and the conductor gave me a look like one would give to a panhandler. I said to him, "Don't worry, I will be cleaning myself up at Edinburgh Station."

He said in his Scottish brogue, "By your accent, matey, we think you could be excused."

After showering and shaving, I felt like a new person. I boarded the train for Newcastle and picked up the *USA Today* to catch up on the college football games. Sitting in a train car, drinking strong black coffee in the late morning to go with an oversized chocolate muffin, and reading the paper was pure luxury compared to having to drive down in a car. No macho stuff for me; I'll let British Rail do my driving.

Julliet met me at Newcastle upon Tyne Station; she looked beautiful and happy to see me. From the station, we walked across the street to an upmarket pub where the specialty was large sandwiches filled with a variety of tasty meats and different types of cheese. That was always a good place to eat and convenient when arriving or leaving Newcastle by train. After lunch, we went to the house she rented and shared with three other university students in a leafy suburb called Jasmond. It was wonderful to see where Julliet lived and to be part of her life, even for a short time.

After going inside and meeting one of her housemates, another nice-looking student, she excused herself for a few minutes. I didn't realize she was going to call Nikki. When Julliet walked back into the room with a phone in her hand, she began to talk into it, saying, "Guess who I have here?" Nikki was thrilled to hear from us both.

Later that evening, we went out to an Italian restaurant close enough to walk to, and her three friends joined us. We could smell the garlic a block away. At the restaurant, I met her favorite waiter and, more importantly, her boyfriend, Dominic. Dom was very polite, well-groomed, and very courteous. After the meal, we went back to Julliet's, with the snow falling, and enjoyed another glass of wine before turning in. Naturally, she asked what I thought of Dom. I replied that I liked him a lot, which must have been quite a relief for her as I'd been pretty tough on her previous boyfriends—none of whom measured up!

I woke up early to have breakfast with Julliet and her friends before walking with them to the university where they were all students working on their various degrees. Snow was lightly falling and starting to cover everything, including us. What a beautiful Christmas-card scene it would have made, with the university—an old, traditional English-looking red-brick building—as a background. She pointed the way to the train station, and we all said good-bye. I had told Julliet that I was off to see Aunt Jacque and Uncle David if the weather permitted. She asked me to say hello to them and their daughter, Victoria, and their son, Meredith. I looked back after walking several yards to see them watching me and then waving again. What a sight to see your daughter all grown up and starting a life full of promise and expectations.

While I was boarding the train, the snow was falling pretty hard. Thankfully, it held off long enough for me to get out of Scotland, which was quite far north. Transferring to other trains at Doncaster and Sheffield could prove to be a little difficult.

I made it to Sheffield and waited for a train to Hathersage, which one British Rail worker said might have to be canceled due to heavy snow on the track. Wanting a backup, I went outside to the taxi rank to see if one of the drivers could get me there. They all said no one would take me since heavy snow was falling in the Peak District. I did not know what to do next, so I went back to the platform where the train was standing. British Rail had changed their minds, and the train was due to leave any minute.

Hooray! I could see everyone on board the short two-car train; I had gotten there just in time. In normal conditions, it should be about a thirty-minute ride to Hathersage. We took off slowly, with me thanking God again; if I hadn't made that train, I would have had to go straight back down to London and miss seeing our friends. I was thinking that when I got to Hathersage Station, I could walk in the snow up the steep hill to the Bevans' house on Hill Lane, which was suitably called Hilltop. All the station signs on the way were covered with snow, so there was no way of telling which station you were at.

After twenty-five minutes, we stopped at a station that looked to me like Hathersage. It's alarmingly funny how small train stations all look so similar covered in snow. I jumped off the train onto a platform deep in snow to brush off the sign, only to find out it was Dore Station—one stop too soon! Getting back on the train, which was full of passengers who all seemed to have their eyes fixed on this lost American, I started brushing off snow. I finally got off at the next stop, which was at last Hathersage Station.

The village was cut off, the roads inaccessible to traffic, and the snow was so deep that it made walking hard. I stopped at the George Hotel in the middle of the village to call the Bevans and tell them I'd arrived. David and Meredith walked down the hill to join me for a pint of beer; it was so good to see them. David brought with him a pair of hiking boots for me with thick socks as my shoes were wet and cold. After we finished our pints, Meredith carried my suitcase, and the three of us made our way up the hill to their home. Jacque had a pot of tea ready as soon as we came through the door. Looking out their large plate glass windows, I could see the panoramic view of the Hope Valley, which was especially beautiful with so much snow. It looked picture-perfect—like a Christmas scene on a card.

We had a very pleasant evening, enjoying a large meal with dark-red Cabernet. Jacque called her friend Nikki to say she'd found somebody she knew in a blizzard and if she would like to speak to him. She could be heard saying that she "sure would!" I told Nikki I was getting closer to Florida but that the snow might be a problem in the morning when I would be catching the train to Sheffield and then on to London. I asked her if she could find someone to pick me up on the dock at Eldred's Marina about 7:00 p.m. I would call her from Atlanta when I got through customs and again when I landed at Sarasota. I said good-bye to my darling and headed off to bed, saying good night and thank you to everyone.

I woke up very early to walk down to the Hathersage train station, creeping out of the house, carefully trying not to wake anyone. The snow was a little less than the previous evening as it must have turned a little warmer during the night. I managed to catch a quick connection to Sheffield and, from there, a direct train to London. I went down the very long escalator for the underground platform to take the tube train to Victoria Station. Then it was back up the equally long escalator to the street level at the Victoria terminal, where I boarded the Gatwick Express train, which left every thirty minutes. After arriving at the Gatwick Airport train terminal, I made my way on the monorail to the north terminal where the travel lodge was a short walk away. Checking in was quick and easy with no one in line at the reception desk. That was rare; it was normally busy all the time.

I couldn't wait to call Nikki to let her know where I was. She was pleased my journey home had started, and she reminded me that I had planned to see our friends Gillian and David before dark.

I said, "Okay, call me back at eight tonight."

That would have given me enough time to do everything. After leaving the hotel, I was on the train again for a one-stop ride to the Three Bridges Station. It was a short walk to the Claytons' house, where they were glad to see me and catch up on news about Nikki and the kids. I was able to see my godson Lawrence and their daughter Katy who both joined in on the conversations. We all had a nice, warm visit, remembering the past twenty-eight years, and after a couple of hours, David kindly drove me back to the hotel. I said good-bye to him and said I hoped that Nikki and I would see them again in February.

Back at the hotel, Tony Pettit of Barton Freight was waiting for me to join him for dinner. I had completely forgotten that we had set that arrangement up the previous week. After an enjoyable dinner, talking mainly about containers and the antique trade, I told him Nikki was calling at eight in about fifteen minutes' time, so I had better get up to my room. He said good night and thanked me for my business. He added, "Lloyd, tell Nikki we will get together again when she is over with you in February."

Nikki called on time; it was so good to talk to her, and it made me really want to get back on the island. I woke up early to have breakfast after a short cold brisk walk to the north terminal. I was finally on my way back to paradise.

CHAPTER EIGHT

🐚 BACK TO LITTLE GASPARILLA ISLAND 🐚

AFTER CHECKING IN for the Delta International flight to Atlanta and going through security and immigration, I went to the duty-free shop for Nikki's perfume, Eternity; that was most important! After having another light breakfast in the business elite lounge of coffee and a sweet roll, it was time to make my way to the newsagents on the way to the gate where I bought several newspapers and the throat lozenges called Lockets, which would keep us going for the next couple of months. Preboarding as a Gold Medallion member gave me a chance to store the luggage and my jacket in the overhead compartment before it got too full.

The first leg of the journey was long, but by reading the newspapers, watching a movie, and working on the two manifests, the time passed quickly. I would often look out the window to see if we were over Greenland or Newfoundland, and then I took a long nap, which made the time go even faster than I had hoped.

Waking up and looking out, I could see the easternmost tip of Newfoundland, a vast area of snow and ice as far as the eye could see, which made me think that we were now over North America and how good it felt inside. The thought of being on the same continent as Nikki, with LGI as an additional bonus and knowing that I'd be there in a few hours, felt wonderful. The

United Kingdom and Harrow, where Nikki grew up, will forever be close to my heart, but Florida will always be home.

We landed at Atlanta, and I hurried off the plane to get in front of most of the passengers so that going through immigration would be quicker; that was in the hope of catching the 3:30 flight. The lines were long, and the custom agent in my queue seemed to be in a slow work mode, but I finally got through and hurried down to catch the airport tram from airside E to airside B. I arrived at the gate as they were just closing the Jetway. I said to myself, *Drat and double drat!* Oh well, I would have to call Nikki to let her know what time I should get to the dock. When I spoke with her, she said Dick would pick me up at Eldred's about 7:00 p.m.

Arriving at Sarasota on time, I was out of the airport quickly with only a carry-on bag to worry about. The car was conveniently parked one hundred yards in front of the terminal. After a short walk, I was on my way down University Parkway to Interstate 75 South. I was at the Eldred's Marina within the hour from the plane landing, managing to be there a few minutes early; even the heavy downpour couldn't deter me from getting to the dock on time. Through the rain and darkness, a boat light was barely visible coming through the narrow channel; it had to be my ride back to the island. I thanked Dick for picking me up in that atrocious weather as he pulled alongside, allowing me to step aboard without tying the boat up, enabling a quick push off from the dock. The wind kept him tight to the dock, which would mean the spray from the waves would be coming into the boat and onto us.

The weather was uncomfortably bad; a cold front was most certainly going through. There were high winds with whitecaps in the Bay. I wished that someone would have told Nikki or me so that I could've stayed in Englewood (probably at our favorite hotel called the Veranda, next to Mama's Restaurant where the food was very Italian and garlicky) to save Dick the risk of running aground in the dark. Dick had shown up on time, and I apologized to him that he had to come out on his boat in such rough weather, but he was pretty tough and shrugged it off, saying he'd been out in worse. We were hitting bottom in the small swells as the Bay was shallow at the best of times, so I went to the front so that the engine would come up a little. I was getting a lot of the spray, but I didn't mind since I would be seeing Nikki in a few minutes.

Despite the rain, Nikki and Napier were on dock 88, standing underneath a big golf umbrella. What a wonderful sight! It felt like I had been away for months instead of a couple of weeks. Nikki had to hold tightly on to Napier as she was trying to jump up for me to stroke her. We all thanked Dick for bringing me over in such foul conditions. It was much better than staying in a hotel in Englewood by myself! Pushing Dick's boat away from the dock was really tough, fighting the wind, but we did it, and finally, I was home again.

The three of us walked back up the lane to our little house, soaking wet but not caring. We soon got some dry clothes on, and Nikki had a steak ready to cook on the grill, which, luckily, was under cover. She said in her lovely English accent, "Sit down on the porch, and I will pour your favorite wine—with ice, of course." We both just stared at each other, so happy to be together again. She said there was lots of news of people wanting to visit us that winter on the island, but we could discuss it all the next day. She continued, "It's more important to get you fed and rested."

Nikki wanted to know all about Julliet and Jonathan and what they had said when I saw them. I told her Jonathan was busy and, unfortunately, couldn't make it to Ladybank to help me. Julliet was fine, and I had met her boyfriend, Dom, who was a really polite young man who could have been another James Bond with his vernacular, good looks, and with his polished accent. Also, Dom was very upright and to the point, with no idle chitchat.

We ate our T-bone steaks, with Napier having one of the bones to chew on. The rain had stopped, so we had a short stroll on the beach smelling the wonderful, fresh salty air. We passed by George's house as he was getting ready to call it a night. After about twenty minutes, Nikki asked if I was tired; I replied that I was indeed, so we headed back. When it was 2:30 a.m. (7:30 a.m., British time), I woke up and asked Nikki if she wanted a cup of coffee. Very sleepily, she declined. I got up and made myself one while Napier also slept. I went for a walk on the beach and could not believe the difference between a frosty cold warehouse in Scotland and being on a warm, white, sandy beach in Florida. The cold front had gone, and it was back to glorious weather. Now I had just a sweatshirt and swimming trunks on; what freedom not to have to wear heavy clothing.

After my walk on the beach, I went down to Peacock Lane to the dock where I sat for half an hour listening to the mullet jump, with dolphins feeding in the dark. I couldn't see them, but I sure could hear the splashing and the blowholes. Going back home to pour another cup of coffee, I realized Nikki would not be stirring for at least another hour, so I sat on the porch listening to the waves crashing onto the beach.

Hearing me in the kitchen and hoping for food, Napier got up to join me after going out on the grass to see what had been around during the night. She wanted to let me know she was glad I was back on the island by brushing up against me, or perhaps she just wanted to be petted. We then went inside to get a little breakfast for the dog, and I heard a faint call for a cup of coffee. After dealing with Napier, I went into the bedroom with both of our coffees.

Nikki said, "Good morning, darling."

I told her it was good to be back in her world. We were both propped up in bed, discussing how the container packing went along with the warehouse accommodations. She wanted to know if our friends, the Bevans, were well and enjoying the snow. I confirmed they were; however, I told her David found it hard to walk the dogs in Derbyshire with two feet of snow on the ground! I then told her they were hoping to come over to see us in February or early March. Nikki said that would be fine because Jim and Jeanette were coming over for Christmas and New Year's for three to four weeks, to have a respite from the Scottish winter. Also, Auntie Philly from Burwell in Cambridgeshire was going to be there at the same time. Nikki said she'd heard from Susan and John Wade from Lake Nottely in Georgia, and they were dropping by in January. Jimetta had called and said she and Lee would also be down to visit.

I told her I thought that was great, and I couldn't wait to show them around the island and introduce them to our newfound friends. That meant that we had about two weeks for ourselves, and then we would be entertaining British friends, Nikki's family, the Delta group, other American friends, plus my family for many weeks.

Nikki got up for breakfast, and then we both had to go over the manifest to get ready to fax Tampa and Austin, Texas. She would type while I broke the list into categories for the custom house broker for them to present to customs. That would take all day, with a few breaks for walking on the beach. It was a really fun endeavor to work in wonderful surroundings. We hoped to be finished by five o'clock because George had invited everyone over for sunset drinks to welcome me back.

Nikki told me we were down to our last gallon of water and would have to think about going over to the mainland or refill several empty gallon jugs down at the state park, which was a half mile down the beach. They have clean city water there to supply the cooler, toilets, and an outside shower. We would walk Napier down, or if Nikki was busy, Napier and I would go down by ourselves. Two full jugs tied to the dog's leash draped around my neck with two in my hands just like before—not too heavy, just a little bit of a workout. We would have to go over before the weekend on the taxi to the marina, where our car was parked, to do a large grocery shop. The last shopping had been done just before I went to Scotland over two weeks ago.

It was decided that we were going to need water, anyway, so a walk down the beach would do us all good. Talking and collecting shells made the walk going there enjoyable, and it went by quickly, but it was not the same coming back, of course, carrying four full gallon jugs in my hands and around my neck. That made it quite difficult to stoop to pick up sharks' teeth, but again, it was not as arduous as loading furniture up and into a sea freight container.

After excusing myself for a much-needed nap (partly due to jet lag), sleeping was no problem, even with mutterings of "Blast!" coming from the kitchen table. It was faintly heard after Nikki made an odd mistake while typing; she was trying to get the manifest list finished in time to walk over to George's at five. We would fax the invoices later with my fee, expenses, and costs of the goods to the respective antique dealers. Nikki woke me about three thirty with a cup of tea to say the typing was almost finished. She thanked me for keeping the number of entries limited by grouping the items. Instead of having two hundred entries on the manifest, we were able to keep them to less than fifty.

I called John in Tampa and Ross in Austin with the total cost. They both were good payers, so the rest of the monies would be in our account by the middle of next week. Nikki was pleased that the trip went so well and that we were making money while living on a barrier island paradise. She indicated that it was time to get washed up in preparation for drinks at sunset on George's deck. We arrived promptly at five and were the first ones there; George was in the house, making a gimlet along with Nikki's scotch and soda. I had brought mine over yet again by not taking the chance if he had remembered my brand. Nikki had to shout (since George was hard of hearing) through the screen door that the service at that bar was going downhill! Nikki could get away with being teasingly rude to George more than anyone else. The rest of us were always more conciliatory since he really was the island elder, especially on Peacock Lane.

George brought our drinks out, and he did have the correct wine for me. We toasted with a "Cheers, George!" from Nikki. "Here's to being on the deck with the best Gulf-front view."

He then said, "Lloyd, I told you not to bring your drink over."

While apologizing to him, saying it won't happen again, June drove up in her cart with Jasper and Bonnie. Napier should have been pleased for the company, but being a black lab, she was more interested in the sausages and crackers on the table. June brought her favorite tipple, as usual, and informed us that her daughter Judy was going to be on the island the coming weekend. And in the same breath, June said in her Texas drawl, "Welcome back, Lloyd, we really did miss you."

I said, "Thank you, you have no idea how glad I am to be back here."

We turned around to see the Sassers pull up, and behind them were Dick and Doris. They all said welcome back while George went back into his house to refresh the drinks. Everyone asked how Scotland was, and I replied, "Very cold and lovely, but it's wonderful to be back in the warm air."

George was saying to all of us that he would like to go fishing again but was unsure if the mackerel had migrated south yet to warmer waters, but he said that we could still cast for mullet off the dock. Nikki then chimed in to say that she and George had toasted my return every sunset while I was gone.

I said, "How nice that was, and every night when I went to bed, I was thinking of you all too."

The sunset was starting to become a colorful spray of hues, with a silvery edge to the clouds that were starting to light up as well as a gold-tinged spray of light that was shining on and broadcasting over the deep blue Gulf waters. The sun seemed to dip so quickly into the water! We all said good night with a casual "See you tomorrow at sunset."

We walked Napier down to the beach one last time before calling it a night. Since everyone had brought plenty of scrumptious snacks, we didn't need to cook. Napier had been fed before going to George's, so Nikki and I could just flop into bed and listen to the waves.

It was easy to get lost in time, not knowing what day it was. Scotland seemed so long ago. Wearing a bathing suit all day gave one a sense of being free instead of the cumbersome clothing that had kept me warm just a week before.

The next morning, Nikki was mumbling something about "Coffee, please," so I was off to make the duchess her morning fix of caffeine and get a little breakfast for Napier. When I brought Nikki her cup, she was sitting up in bed with a notepad, making a list of all the friends and family who were going to be visiting us over the next two months. It was now confirmed: Jim and Jeanette would be there for four weeks over Christmas, New Year's, and into January. Auntie Philly would also be there for two weeks over the same holiday period.

There were only two bedrooms, so we thought that Auntie Philly, a.k.a. Phil, would not mind sleeping on the couch. I remembered Philly getting a little bored in the second week whenever she went anywhere with us. I reminded Nikki about our experience in Tenerife after walking back from the resort town; her verbal assault on the area was "If I have to walk through another effing building site, I'm going to snuff myself."

Nikki started giggling, saying that was her all over. We hoped it would be different on the island.

The next week went by very quickly. I did a lot of fishing while Nikki did the *Daily Telegraph* crossword book or the ones in the *Englewood Herald* or sometimes *Sun* puzzles and when someone came from Tampa and brought us the *Tribune*. We also walked the beach three or four times a day, looking for sharks' teeth and sand dollars as well as reading a lot of books from the island library. Life was full; we were never bored or looking for something to do. The days flew by.

Lee and Jimetta were picking up the McGills from Tampa Airport the next evening then driving down with Bill and his wife Dee (old friends of theirs from Tampa) in their motor home the following day. They would be catching the Eldred's taxi over to the island. They would be arriving early and depart late afternoon, probably before dark, leaving the McGills with us. Now we had chores to do before the invasion of the Scots!

We gave Jimetta the shopping list, which would save us the task of spending half a day going to the grocery store. My task was to clear the porch, which was always an enjoyable chore. To look up every now and then and see the Gulf waters meant it wasn't like work at all. We would take a break every hour for a cup of tea or walk on the beach while asking each other what we thought our guests' reaction would be to the place. We both agreed, you either love it or can't handle it because of the remoteness.

Tommy's beach house was pretty basic; the fridge was from the 1960s and had rust spots all over it. The stove wasn't much better and was the same vintage, with two of the four rings not working. Only one appliance could be used at one time in the kitchen, or a fuse would blow. There was old-fashioned pecan paneling throughout, with the wall between the two bedrooms the width of the smaller size of a two-by-four, and no installation in any of the walls.

A quiet evening would give us a chance to rest up in preparation for the next four weeks. It was going to be a busy time with loads of company, especially over the holidays when there would be many island parties to attend; several early invitations had already arrived. We walked to the beach with our cocktails, waiting for the sunset. George was on his deck with Glen Kennedy, a friend of his from New Jersey who had a house farther down on the beach. Glen's in-laws, the Yungels, built one of the original houses on the island and were the reason the Geiers were introduced to this unique paradise. George waved to us, and we raised our glasses and said cheers as the sun disappeared. We said that we would see him the following day for drinks and to introduce our Scottish friends to him.

Back home, we grilled lamb chops on the barbecue, and while I was waiting for the charcoal to start up, we poured ourselves a glass of wine. Napier was now sniffing the tree, wondering if a varmint had visited while we were on the beach earlier. Sitting on the swing and enjoying the sea breeze, we talked about what to do in the morning. Nikki suggested we go to the park for more water, but I said that Napier and I would go while she stayed to tidy up and listen for the phone in case the group was going to be earlier or later than planned.

We ate our dinner with our usual enjoyment, and then it was time to settle down for a well-deserved night's sleep. Napier heard a noise outside; it was probably either a raccoon or opossum, and she wouldn't settle down until she was let out. So I took the torch, and we discovered a raccoon on the porch, feeding on crumbs from supper and bits of potato chips. Then as we went back to bed, I whispered to Napier, "You will have a long day tomorrow annoying Jimetta and the rest of the company, so you better get some sleep." We all had a good night and awoke at our usual time of around 5:30 a.m. full of great expectations of having our friends stay with us.

At just before six, the drip coffee was on, and I got Napier's breakfast. Then I took Nikki her cup of coffee and asked her if she wanted to go see the sunrise on the dock. She responded with "Give me a few minutes to get up and put my shorts on." Napier and I were ready to go, and within minutes, we were all walking down the sandy lane toward the Bay. There were several types of paw prints from a number of different critters; it was fun trying to figure them out.

We got to the dock just as the sun was peeking under the Boca Grande Causeway drawbridge. What a bright array of colors—absolutely stunning! Anyone who has ever witnessed sunrise from LGI will treasure the sight forever. One of Nikki's favorite songs was "Morning Has Broken," a very moving spiritual hymn that did epitomize the scene. We just sat on the edge of the dock with our feet almost in the Bay for twenty minutes or so. It was then time to go back to get some toast and a refill of coffee.

On our walk back, we saw June letting her dogs Jasper and Bonnie out into the yard. Napier ran up to say hello to them. I told her about the visitors from Scotland coming in for four weeks, and she said she couldn't wait to meet them. I said that we should all meet on George's deck that evening. June suggested that we take her golf cart to haul our visitors' luggage up the lane when they arrive. We thanked her very much. As we walked back to the house, we again said to each other how nice the island people were; they wanted everyone to love LGI as much as they did. We did feel that we were living a wonderful life. Nikki used a word to describe us: *bon vivants*. While I agreed, I also wanted to look up the word in the dictionary as soon as we got back to the house.

With breakfast finished, Napier and I were off to fetch four gallons of water and look for sharks' teeth as we went. We started to amble on our way when I heard Nikki say, "Lloyd, no looking for sharks' teeth. We have too much to do!"

We were gone for over an hour. On my return, I swept the porch again. Nikki came out with a cup of tea, and I mentioned to her that the roof was deep in pine needles again. I noticed that it hadn't rained yet, but when it did, they may not be good for the asphalt tiles. Nikki thought that if I give Jim a few days to rest up and recover from jet lag, then he could hold the ladder while I went up to sweep them off.

While we were on the porch sipping the tea, the phone rang. It was Jimetta, saying they were about one hour away from Eldred's

Marina. We frantically looked over the house to see what, if anything, was needed to be done. We ticked off the list that the carpet was vacuumed, that the kitchen and bathroom floors were mopped; however, the screens on the windows were still dirty. We had been afraid of taking them out to clean, just in case they fell apart. Lastly, Nikki said that we should dust the tops of the fans as they were covered in dirt and dust. It took us forty-five minutes to wash the blades—having company certainly gets the job done!

We walked down to June's and picked up the golf cart, and then it was off to the dock. When the buggy was backed up to the walkway, we were finally ready for their arrival.

CHAPTER NINE

 THE BRITISH INVASION

T HE THREE OF us were again sitting on the dock of the
Bay, trying to pick out the Eldred's taxi coming through
the channel from the mainland. We both saw it at the same time
and shared the excitement of knowing that our friends Jim and
Jeanette were really going to be here soon; even Napier sensed
that something good was going to happen. We couldn't wait to
see their faces when they saw Peacock Lane for the first time and
walk through the canopy of trees that would seem like a tropical
jungle to them.

As the boat got closer to us, they started to wave enthusiastically;
we waved back, and Napier was wagging her tail like crazy.
I'm sure she could recognize the taxi, which usually meant that
whoever was on board was most likely going to add to her life
in the form of an extra petting or scrap of food. Soon it was
pulling alongside the end of the dock, with everyone inside the
boat looking very happy to be there; the big smiles on their faces
summed up the atmosphere.

We all gave hugs and kisses as they climbed up on the dock,
saying, "Good to see you again!"

Jeanette's opening remark was "How in the world did you find
this place?"

Sam, the boat captain, said to me, "Little Gasparilla will never be the same again. The British have taken over without firing a shot!"

Nikki then said, "Sam, we have another wave of Brits coming in the next two weeks and then again five weeks after that." He said that was way too much for him to take in, and we all laughed as he pulled away.

We started down the walkway to the golf cart with all the McGills' gear and the lunch that had been prepared by Jimetta and Dee. Lee was carrying a box of cigars for all the guys. Then it was a short walk to the beach house; that is, except for Dee, Jimetta, and Bill, who traveled on the cart with the luggage and provisions.

As we ambled along behind the cart, Nikki and I were looking at Jim and Jeanette's faces to catch their expressions; once we got to the overgrown thicket, which made a short tunnel, we could hear the slight roar of the surf. They were very game and seemed to take it all in with just a little trepidation. As we got closer to the beach house, suddenly, the Gulf came into full view. "Wow!" they all said. "What a magnificent sight—the blue water seems endless." We think they knew that they were in a time and place so few have experienced. Then came the real test: the inside of Tommy's beach house! Jeanette said it was very interesting and "Not exactly Harrow, is it, Nikki?"

"No," she replied, "pavements are as rare as streetlights, and you wouldn't want to use the well water to mix with your scotch!"

Jim said at the same time, "But it beats camping by a long way!"

Everyone helped to get the luggage and all the food inside. Dee had made chicken cacciatore for supper, and Jimetta and Lee had brought Cuban sandwiches for lunch, along with a few bottles of champagne to wash it down. Everyone put the stuff away, and then we were all ready to sit down for lunch; the sandwiches were huge and delicious. We toasted us all being there together, and Bill said that this was definitely his type of place, with lots of places to fish. Jimetta, Lee, and Dee were less enthusiastic because they realized that there were no cars or roads and nowhere to go shopping or go out to eat other than by boat. However, after lunch, everyone was anxious to go for a walk on the beach.

As we stepped onto the sand, there was nobody else to be seen as far as the eye could see—north or south. Everyone said they could not believe that it was so deserted after being used to the beaches around Tampa, Clearwater, and St. Pete, which were always so crowded. We walked for about an hour south, passing some nice-looking beach houses but without seeing anyone. Our visitors loved watching the seabirds flying over the water, especially the pelicans, which were the most amazing of them all. Nikki demonstrated how to look for sharks' teeth, and the girls collected some beautiful shells.

Then we returned to the house and sat on the porch with cups of tea and relaxed for a while. After a short doze (for some of us), we all decided to go back to the beach, but that time, we'd go north to see the sand dunes. We didn't get all the way to the park because it was time to go back for supper, a little early because of the Tampa crowd having to catch the water taxi at four o'clock back to the marina. Dee warmed up the chicken dish, which was served with salad and garlic bread—delicious!

We all had lots to eat, so a walk to the dock was a good way to work it off. We waddled down there well in time because Sam the boat captain was sometimes early if it was a slow day. We were right: he was already there waiting for us, hoping to get back in time for another delivery to the island. As they boarded the boat and slowly pulled away from the dock, we waved good-bye to Lee, Jimetta, Bill, and Dee; then Jeanette and Jim and Nikki and I went back to the house to fix cocktails, ready for sunset.

We could see June and George on his deck, waving for us to come over as we were a bit late. When we were settled, Nikki introduced our Scottish friends; June and George mentioned that we had almost missed the sun going down, but luckily, we were just in time. Jim and Jeanette were delighted to see it and to be in such a glorious place, as they both conveyed to all of us. The sun was down, but it was still warm, and the sky was filled with hues of orange and turquoise, so we stayed a little longer.

George said, "I guess, since you are from Scotland, you'd like a scotch."

Jim said, "That would be appreciated, George."

Then Nikki, Jeanette, and I got our orders in. June, of course, had brought hers with her, as is her wont. The girls got up to help George after a few minutes. He was also preparing hors d'oeuvres of crackers with a piece of pepperoni on top—George's main sunset snack. We held the screen door open for the three bringing out our refreshments—a little later than was usual.

We finally left George's for our place in order to cook barbecue steaks on the grill for our supper. The grill was ready since we had lit the charcoal before going across the lane for the welcoming party. The girls were getting the salad together while Jim and I were cooking the steaks. We really didn't need to eat again, but starting their holiday with a barbecue was a Florida tradition for the four of us. That was a lot of food served in one day, but we had enough leftovers to last several more days.

We had one more walk after supper to the dock with Napier. After standing there for a few minutes to take in the beautiful sights and sounds, we headed back home to turn in after a very full day. Jeanette had a shower, and she called out to Jim to see what he could do to turn the smelly brown shower water to something that would clean her instead of making her dirtier! When Jim came out of the bathroom, he was laughing, as was Jeanette from behind the closed bathroom door. We apologized while telling them that was the best it was going to be and added that we were getting used to it, as we hoped they would. Jeanette emerged from a very quick shower, still laughing as only Jeanette can do. We all went to bed weary and tired—even the dog.

Jeanette was the first to wake as she was still on Scottish time, and she took the opportunity to become accepted by Napier, who was jumping up to greet her. The dog managed to scratch Jeanette's legs, which she was naturally not very happy about. Her first war wounds on LGI! Little did we know then that more was to come from that pesky dog. Jeanette took her and Jim's tea into the bedroom, probably to get away from an overly exuberant lab looking for someone new to play with. I then took Nikki a cup of coffee to have in bed and then gave Napier her breakfast. Nikki thought it would be a good idea to get in and out of the bathroom before the line of bathers gathered. A simple breakfast for everyone was toast, English muffins with jam, local strawberries, along with cups of tea or coffee put out on the kitchen table since there was very little counter space. Napier was now ready for a walk while everyone else slowly emerged.

The beach again was empty, with lots of newly washed up shells. We were gone for at least forty minutes, with Napier looking for old fish or something worse to eat, as most black labs seemed to do. I told Napier it was time to go back, so she mustn't aggravate the guests anymore; needless to say, she still needed a lot more training. She never listened to what anyone said, especially when they were holding a sandwich or a biscuit in their hands. I believe all black labs are addicted to food—at least, all the ones that I had come across were, whether in America, Scotland, or England. On the other hand, you would be hard pressed to find a dog with a nicer nature. Napier proved to be a loyal and true companion until she died at fourteen years old.

We couldn't wait to spend time with Jim and Jeanette and show them what we had discovered on LGI. There was a lot to do in the short time they were there. That day, we all walked toward the south end of the island where a skinny red Hungarian Vishnu ran down his steps to tell Napier that that was his part of the beach. Since

Napier was much larger, the red dog decided that she wanted to just play, but Napier soon got agitated and could not do anything about it since the other dog was so quick.

The Vishnu's owner called, "Sophie, come back!" We figured that was her name, and we waved to the man up at a stilt house. He seemed very friendly and came down to introduce himself. His name was Buddy Gains, and we would find out, interestingly enough, that his son was Rowdy Gains, the great Olympic swimmer. (We were told later he was named after the Western character Rowdy Yates).

We went back to the house for a cup of tea and to plan our next excursion. Sitting on the porch, gazing out periodically to watch the waves, pelicans, and sandpipers, Nikki mentioned to our guests that the island was far different from the Indian Rocks area where we usually vacationed. She said we would quite understand if they felt a bit marooned and wanted to go back to Indian Rocks, where there are many restaurants and certainly more to do.

Jim said, "No, in fact, we can't believe how great it is here without cars or noise of people and traffic."

Nikki and the McGills started the telegraph crossword with printed copies off the fax machine, and Napier and I went for a nap early, hoping lunch would be ready when we arose.

After lunch, we walked to the dock. A boat was at the next dock to the south, and a man and woman were bringing items up to their house, their porch being connected by a walkway to the dock. They introduced themselves as Bob and June Shirley. We all thought they were about our age and were very friendly, with Southern Floridian drawls. After a short but pleasant visit, they invited us down to their place for five o'clock cocktails, and we said, "Thank you very much, we will see you then." They were most enamored with our friends' Scottish accents along with Nikki's posh London one. We went back to the house to get ready for our second cocktail party in two nights! We hoped George wasn't going to be put out with us missing a sunset on his deck.

Someone said, "Who is going to have a smelly shower first?" And the other three said, "Do we have to?" So I took my first and very short one, to leave enough warm water for the others. We left at exactly five. George was on his deck with three other people. He saw us go the opposite way while waving to him as we walked down the lane. Everything turned out just right. He wasn't slighted as we were not rude by not going by.

Bob and June were all smiles to see us, and Bob extended his hand in friendship as we stepped up onto their front porch. June told us of some history of these parts of LGI. She said Peacock Lane was named after her parents, as Peacock was her surname. She pointed to a house in the middle of a bunch of oak trees across Peacock Lane that had been her parents' house but now belonged to the Sassers, who had bought it to use as a getaway place in the summers. They all lived in the middle of Florida, where it was a little hotter than the island (mainly because of the Bay and Gulf breezes). They asked us if we would like to go to another island just one hour south, where there was a famous restaurant. That area was known as Cabbage Key, and June said the reason for the name is that a type of palm tree grows there that produces a cabbagelike vegetable from the heart of the palm. We all agreed, and Bob said, "How about this Saturday, around 11:00 a.m.?"

We all confirmed with a very excited "Yes!"

We then went back to get the evening meal ready when Jeanette said that they had met more friends in the last three days than they had in the first three years of moving to Alyth, Scotland!

Saturday was finally here, and it was off to Cabbage Key with Bob and June. During the twenty-minute ride to Boca Grande Pass, the water was a bit rough, especially just past the old phosphate loading docks. Bob told us that it was always choppy because there were two rivers merging into the large pass; at both high- and low-tide changes, the water could be treacherous. He also said that the area had some of the best fishing for tarpon (a game fish) as well as sharks, especially world-record hammerheads, along with king and Spanish mackerel.

We arrived at Cabbage Key after another thirty minutes, with Nikki looking slightly ill—she never did like being on a boat, which was a little crazy when you lived on an island, but she braved it when she had to. We had just passed another island called Useppa, home only to the rich and famous, where the yachts are larger than the houses!

We tied up to the restaurant dock, walking past a very large mound of shells. Bob told us that the Indians made that mound by throwing used conch, clam, or oyster shells there. We all walked the trail meandering through the salt marshland palm trees as well as other types of undisturbed native plants. The interior of the restaurant was rustic, to say the least. Seafood was their specialty—any way you wanted it cooked! The food was indeed excellent and plentiful; there was enough left over to take home.

On the way back, we saw lots of dolphins, along with ospreys and pelicans; it was such a treat for us all. The birds were seen for the full hour of going back, and seeing our enjoyment, June asked if they could take us fishing on Monday. Jim told her he belonged to a fishing club in Scotland and was more than ready to accept the invitation. Nikki gracefully declined. We asked what we could pack and for how long a day it was going to be. They said to pack enough liquids to be able to stay hydrated for approximately four hours. The mackerel were moving south, so it could be a good day to catch our supper. We got back to the Shirleys' dock and helped them tie up their boat, and then it was back to the beach house for us.

There was a message on the answering machine; Nikki's aunt Phyllis was arriving the following Monday for a two-week holiday. I would go to Tampa Airport to get her, so I suggested that Nikki make a shopping list for enough provisions for a week. The fishing trip was still good for the rest of our company, and Nikki said she would stay home with the dog and clean up the house. I noted that it would be a while before Nikki got on another boat after that day's trip because the Boca Grande Pass was a little scary in Bob's small boat. It was all settled then; we would all do our own thing Monday except when it came to five o'clock on someone's deck or porch.

June Hicks walked up to ask if we wanted to go to her house that evening or if we would like to watch the sunset from our place as the views were better there; in that case, she said that she would come down. June said to Nikki, "Your friends from Scotland are very nice, with a quiet disposition—not like some of our loud, boisterous Americans!"

Nikki was pleased to hear that and was really proud to call them friends. Jeanette said that it seemed that they had been there much longer than four days, and she was amazed at all the people they had met. Nikki went across the lane to ask George over at five, and I knew that he couldn't turn her down, even at eighty; there was something in those piercing blue eyes of his and the dark tan that an attractive lady could still turn his head. He was quite enamored with her and her schooled English accent.

We were almost all set for another gathering. I went down to Bob and June's to ask them up, but they said they were already going out for supper; however, they would love a rain check. I said that would be fine and that we would definitely see them the following day. I then went back to the house to get ready. We all asked one another who was going to brave the shower first. Jim volunteered, with Jeanette next in line. Nikki would follow, and I would go last. If there would be any hot water left, it would have been a bonus!

It was almost five, and our hors d'oeuvres were nachos with salsa—not bad, for marooned people on an island. That evening, everyone knew one another, and we all said it was good to get together again. Dick and Doris drove up to George's with Jessie and Sally in the golf cart, and George yelled at them to join us. We had plenty of snacks to go round. Our porch was full of islanders, and we really felt we belonged now—what a great feeling that was.

Ed and Louise had smoked mullet that he smoked on his barrel grill. That was the first time the McGills had eaten any type of mullet. It was surely strong, but very tasty, and there was enough so that we needn't cook that evening. The sun went down, but everyone stayed to chat for about another hour. June popped home to put together another of her special gin and tonics. Eventually, everyone went home, and after the ladies cleaned up, there was nothing to do except walk Napier on the beach. As always, she loved chasing elusive sandpipers that would circle back around, squawking to protest her being there—I was always amused at the sight. Soon we went back home to go to bed; we were all extremely tired from the boat trip and the party. The bed felt so comfortable. *No trouble sleeping tonight,* I thought to myself!

We woke up Sunday morning to hear Jim and Jeanette making coffee. Napier wanted out of the bedroom to see what was going on in the kitchen. She jumped up on Jeanette, and I noticed that it was never Jim who got the attention when we heard "The damn dog scratched me again!"

Oh dear—I knew how much it could hurt, but of course, Napier didn't realize that.

Nikki was making our coffee, and the McGills were on the porch with the door open. The temperature was in the high sixties, and everyone remarked on how pleasant the weather was. Our dog was still pestering them, and Jeanette asked me to control her, so I told Napier in a harsh voice to lie down, which she did, but only for a few seconds—though she did understand "Stay!"

Why was she so naughty? I asked myself. She was such a cute little puppy when we adopted her, and now, at over one hundred pounds of solid dog, she was full of mischievous behavior because of being spoiled all her life by both of us. We were reaping what we sowed!

The Duchess of Harrow had her coffee and would appear in the next ten minutes with our plans for the day. I'm sure the Sunday roast would be the top priority for discussion that morning. The chicken was thawing and in the fridge already.

Everyone had their toast, and Napier was waiting for Nikki's unwanted crust. We discussed what to have with the roast chicken, and it seemed that mashed potatoes were a favorite, with vegetables and gravy. Breakfast and Sunday lunch had been taken care of, so now we were ready for a walk to the north end of the island, with a stop at the state park to fill up on water jugs. We should be able to carry six gallon jugs back between four adults as well as keep an eye on the dog. That would be a new venture for most of the others; the plus side is that we would work off a couple of pounds before indulging in our lunch.

Going to the park, we kept up a fairly good pace, but coming back, we just ambled along with our freight of fresh mains water. When we arrived home, someone put the kettle on for a cup of tea with a piece of fruitcake.

We made plans to go to the little island library where the books were mainly paperback novels that people had donated. There were probably close to five hundred books in inventory, where one could take out and bring back anytime. We all looked at the choices and picked out a few books each. After our return, Nikki and Jeanette started cooking the Sunday roast while I peeled potatoes before retreating to the bedroom for my usual early-afternoon rest. I emerged to find the gang of three having a prelunch glass of wine, and as I was a sociable fellow, they insisted on pouring me my favorite Cabernet. I asked, "To what deplorable, lovely behavior have I descended to? Honestly!

Drinking in the middle of the day! Oh well, once a week isn't so terrible."

The Sunday roast was excellent, and we all demolished the offering. Even Napier had a little chicken skin, and then we all collapsed on the porch with a pot of strong coffee. The consensus was that we were all too full to have a walk just then, but maybe in an hour or two. The other three fell asleep, but Napier wanted to know what was going on at the beach, so we crept off the porch so as not to wake anyone. We had had our sleep earlier, so we were ready to chase birds and look for sharks' teeth.

We were back in just over an hour to find them all awake. Jim said he had been for a short walk, and the other two said they were ready for another one. We all agreed to see what was happening on the Bay, so off we all trotted toward the dock.

Bob and June stopped to talk to us, and we let them know that only Jim and Jeanette would be going fishing with them the next day since I would be going to the Tampa Airport to pick up Nikki's aunt Phyllis. We used up another hour talking while sitting on the dock, which we now called George's Dock. His boat was always there on the right-hand side just below the right T out, to give more dock area jutting out in the front.

We went back to the house to do the washing up; there were plenty of pots and pans, silverware, plates, and glasses. The girls said that they would wash while the boys would dry, and then they would put everything away. Once it was all done, we were ready for another strong cup of coffee to reinvigorate us.

The three of them took out the crossword they couldn't finish the previous day. Nikki asked me to call the kids in the UK. Julliet was fine, but there was no answer from Jonathan's again. No doubt, he was having a good time with his university friends in Aberdeen.

It was almost five and time to meander over to George's deck, where we could see him sitting alone. We decided to fix our own drinks to give him the evening off, and we went over the soft deep sand where it piled up when it got windy and settled by his little detached golf cart garage. There was a ramp there going up to his deck. It really was a slog to plow through the heavy sand. Jim asked what kind of structure or architectural design George's house was, with his deck being a wraparound. The beach house was more round than octagonal, designed to take a gale-force wind, which would blow around it instead of through it, a prefab probably from the 1950s, but with a beautiful beach front setting.

George wanted to know all about Jim and Jeanette, what they did, where they lived in Scotland, and most of all, how they came to know us. As the sun went down, it was a little cloudy, so there was not much to see. We said good night to George as it was going to be a very busy day the next day. We told George that we would soon have yet another English lady for him to meet—Nikki's auntie Philly. He said he was really looking forward to entertaining her there on the deck.

We were all getting weary and planning to have an early night, so I took Napier for a short walk then back to the beach house. Before retiring, we all said what a fantastic day it had been.

CHAPTER TEN

 AUNT PHYLISS ARRIVES

I WOKE UP early Monday morning, realizing I was going to have a busy day. The water taxi was picking me up at nine as I had to do some shopping before picking Philly up at Tampa Airport at 3:00 p.m. She was going to be exhausted, traveling from Cambridge and staying overnight in London in order to catch the early flight to New York, then transferring to a flight to Tampa. She had stayed with her friend Josie O'Leary, whom she used to hang out with in the late 1930s and '40s while enduring the bombings in London of World War II. The tales we had heard from those two wonderful ladies over the years were inspiring, with their attitude toward that time in history being young girls working in a high-street department store selling fashions, dating their young men, and going to the pub between sheltering in the underground rail systems when the sirens would sound out warnings all over London.

The plan was to be back to Eldred's for the taxi at five thirty that evening. With a bit of luck, we would make sunset. The shopping was done and in the cooler, the traffic was good on the highway, and Philly's plane was on time. We were right on schedule as we pulled away from Tampa Airport.

Traveling back on the interstate over the Sunshine Skyway Bridge, I hoped that she would enjoy the magnificent coastal views if the jet lag wasn't getting to her too much. She did like looking at the water, but more importantly, she wanted to know how Nikki was doing and if she was she enjoying the solitude of the island. I said she was very much, and then I asked her how the flight was and how Josie was doing. She said the flight was really good, and Josie was still flying out to the Orient and Egypt, buying women's fashions for her company. I then asked about her husband Bert and their two sons, Laurie and Robert. She replied that Bert was still as ornery as ever, and the boys were doing great in both their careers as well as in their family lives. The jet lag finally kicked in, and Philly nodded off for about an hour; she woke up as we were pulling into Eldred's a few minutes early—perfect timing.

Sam was waiting to take us over and said to Nikki's auntie as he helped her into the water taxi, "I was warned that you were on your way."

Laughingly, Philly replied, "I am used to comments like that, especially from Lloyd."

I said with a grin, "Oh yes, many times over the last twenty-eight years."

When we were in the middle of Gasparilla Bay, she said, "You would think there would be a bridge to this place."

Sam told her, "Absolutely not, and we don't want one!"

The whole gang was at the dock to meet us, including Napier. As Sam was pulling away, he said, "Good luck, Lloyd!" June and George were there in their golf carts to get us back in time to see the sun go down.

Nikki was very glad to see her aunt, and everyone else seemed pleased to meet her; even Napier was excited, as she usually was when someone new arrived. Philly was tired from her long trip but still wanted to see the sun setting over the water. She knew how lovely it was as she'd been to Florida on the Gulf Coast a few times with her companion Lawrence (after her separation from Bert) and also on several trips with her old friend Josie.

We all piled the shopping in and let the ladies ride on the two carts. Jim, Napier, and I walked fast behind in order to off-load the luggage and the provisions as time was running out. We made it to the house with five minutes to spare before the sun would disappear behind the horizon. Philly was very happy to be there, and catching the sunset was a big bonus for her. She had a traditional cup of tea (as the British so often do when they arrive somewhere), and we all had our usual drinks and on the porch with the golf buggy owners, June and George.

Everything had been put away, and Nikki had supper already prepared. We couldn't wait to hear how the fishing went with Jim and Jeanette. But that wouldn't be for a little while yet as it was still mayhem with so many people on the porch and in the kitchen. Nikki whispered a thank-you to me for picking up Philly at Tampa Airport. I, of course, replied that she was delightful all the way back and that she even liked the Eldred's boat taxi as she took in the view of the Bay with LGI in the distance. Everyone agreed that we should go ahead and serve dinner as we were all getting hungry. It was going to be an early night for me again since my nap had not been on the schedule that day. After dinner, the group of us adjourned to the porch with a cup of tea.

Jim finally had the chance to tell us that the trip to Cabbage Key was great; they had docked the boat and walked the nature trail that went around the perimeter of the island, through the swampland that was home to a lot of Florida plant life and birds. The fishing was also good, trolling for mackerel, and several dolphins followed the boat for quite a way, hoping for a handout of fresh fish. Jeanette said she was cold and had to huddle inside Bob's boat, reading to stay warm while the rest of them did the fishing.

Napier still wanted a walk before going to bed, and of course, Philly wanted to turn in early, so that would mean us all going to bed at the same time so that she could sleep on the couch. Nikki and I talked as we lay there, and I had to remind her that the walls were very thin, so we whispered to each other. That day was the first relaxing one in a week for her because she had been by herself with Napier, who mainly stayed on the porch while she cleaned up the house. Nikki said it was good that Philly had made it to Florida at her age, traveling alone, and I agreed. We said that we would have to watch Napier to make sure that she didn't jump up on auntie, and then off to sleep we went.

Next morning came too quickly, as it does sometimes when you love sleep as much as I do. Thinking I had to put Napier out before Philly woke up, I crept into the living room to find her up and dressed with a cup of tea.

"Morning, Lloyd," she whispered. "Is Nikki awake?"

I replied, "Not until she's had her first cup of coffee, and that would be ready soon."

I put Napier outside with her breakfast, warning Philly to watch out for Napier jumping up to get attention, as she had already clawed Jeanette twice; I reinforced the importance of being careful. The McGills were rising, and Nikki was drinking her coffee; all was well in the beach house so far. For the next twelve days, Nikki would have all her time taken up by her aunt, but that was fine by me, for it would give me time to go fishing or cast the net for mullet. We would likely all converge at lunch, sunset, and evening meal, and I was sure Philly would organize games to play—probably Nikki's favorite, which was Country County.

That evening, we were all invited to George's deck for drinks at sunset, and the whole clan was there to meet Philly. She was in her element with all the interest shown by our new friends, asking her about her life story. Especially what it was like during the war in London, when Hitler was bombing for six weeks nonstop. She talked about her friend Josie O'Leary and of them having quite a bit of fun even though it was wartime, telling George to remember that they were both very young at the time! When the bombers came over, they had to take refuge in the underground train tunnels, which brought all the Londoners together. Coincidentally, George's older brother Fred had recuperated in a London hospital after sustaining a spinal injury from a shrapnel wound at the Battle of Normandy during that same time. When we had had enough of war stories, we went back to our beach house to have dinner.

Nikki and Philly got the ink pens and paper, ready to play games. I wanted to go to bed, but I knew I would have to play at least one game before being excused for the night. After managing that, I was glad to be lying in bed almost asleep, feeling I had just escaped! I woke up early the next morning feeling refreshed, along with Napier, so I took her outside for a walk to let everyone sleep in. We walked the beach to the south then out to the middle of the island, working our way to our dock. After being away for over an hour, I realized Nikki would want her coffee, and I got back to find Philly on the porch with her tea. I asked if she'd heard any noise from any of the others, and she said, "No, but it's a good time to put the pot on before they all wake up."

Jim and Jeanette were getting into island mode by sleeping in most mornings. I made toast for Philly and myself before taking Nikki her coffee; she was just waking up, so the timing was perfect. She told me that last night, it had been decided that they were all going to the mainland to go shopping and asked if I would like to go. Napier needing my company was my excuse for not joining them, and I asked her what time she would like the boat taxi to pick them up. Nikki said that we had to wait until the others got up to make that decision.

Napier and I went for another walk to give everyone a chance to make coffee and toast and, more importantly, decide when to make the crossing because the taxi might need an hour's notice. As I walked, I was thinking that I'd be glad to be alone for some peace and quiet. When I got back to the house, I made sure Nikki had the keys to the Jeep and said I would help take water jugs, coolers, and essentials to the dock.

Jim said, "Lloyd, are you sure you would rather stay on the island than go shopping?"

"Quite sure, Jim. This way, there will be more room in the car for you guys as well as all the purchases."

Off they went, waving good-bye from the boat taxi; Napier had tried to board as she wanted to go as well but settled for staying with me.

Back at the house, I was so happy to have it to myself. I made a sandwich and a cup of tea then went to take a nap while listening to talk radio. Everyone's hero on the island was Rush Limbaugh, and I wanted to listen to what he was all about. After living and working in the United Kingdom since 1981, he was new to me, but what he said made sense and was good entertainment, with plenty food for thought. At least it made me feel good enough to easily fall asleep. What a luxury it was to have a nap in the early afternoon with the soft sea breezes infiltrating the bedroom.

After Napier and I woke up, I took a cup of tea out to the porch. George drove by in his golf cart and stopped to ask if I could give him a hand to clean the bottom of his boat engine by scraping the barnacles off. I said that I would be glad to; he told me to wear some old clothes because it was a smelly, messy job. I said that all my clothes are old, and with that, we both had a laugh. I jumped on the cart to ride down with him; Napier got in and sat on the floor while I tried to position my feet around her.

George said with a smile, "I didn't invite her," and I could tell that George really did like our dog.

I was brushing and scraping for only about thirty minutes until George was satisfied that the propeller would run better. The barnacles were like little clams that attach themselves to any kind of surface that is in the saltwater. Every time I scraped a row of them off, they would squirt a smelly, watery substance toward us.

George wasn't flexible enough to sit on the dock while scraping, so he just gave the orders. It only took half an hour for the work to be deemed satisfactory to the boss.

We went back to the house on George's golf cart. We couldn't see Napier to give her a ride, but when we approached the house, she was sitting on the porch. As he dropped me off, he said that he would see me at five. I warned him that there would be a lot of us, and he said as he drove off, "Good, the more the merrier!"

After stripping off the dirty, fishy clothes and throwing them out onto the porch, it was time for a smelly shower! Then I was ready to go down to the dock to meet the gang. Napier and I got there just when the taxi was pulling alongside.

Nikki said, "Good timing, my darlings. We do have an awful lot of shopping." I asked Nikki if they all had fun, and she said, "Yes, it was good to go to the mainland for a change."

For her, it had been almost a month without getting off the island. She told me that Jim and Jeanette bought lunch for all of them, and then she asked me if I'd had a good time by myself. I told her I'd helped George with boat cleaning and that he wanted us all to join him at five, so we'd all better hurry to get our island-cocktail gear on. When we all reached the house, Nikki saw that my dirty and smelly old clothes were on the porch. She said that maybe I should rinse them outside at the fish-cleaning sink.

It was a miracle that we were ready to start our walk down to George's right at five o'clock. He was waving and waiting for us to arrive, and there was cheese and crackers with sausage to snack on, like always. We all had our drinks in hand as we walked up his ramp to enjoy another beautiful sunset (except Nikki and Philly, as George would insist on making theirs).

During the conversation about Philly's trip on the water taxi, Nikki made a comment about how much she disliked traveling on boats. George replied, "What on earth are you doing on an island with no bridges if you don't like boats?"

"It's a lovely place where we can stay for three months, and all thanks to Tommy and Amber, Lloyd's extended family, for free!" said Nikki. "Plus, Lloyd has found his old Florida dream place which reminds him of where he grew up in the very rural Hillsborough County, with its sandy roads leading to the Alafia River swimming hole."

Old George said gruffly, "That sounds like a good reason to be here, but you didn't mention escaping the cold in North Georgia during the harshest part of winter."

Nikki giggled. "Slipped my mind, George!"

George said he was going over the following day to get his haircut, if anyone would like a lift. Nikki said, "Lloyd would probably like to go with you since he also needed one."

After another fantastic sunset, we all left to fix our suppers. When we got to the house, Nikki said, "Darling, I thought it would be good for you to help George tie the boat up on the marina and carry his shopping tomorrow, as he seems to be shuffling a lot."

What a good idea she had; I sure wish I'd thought of it myself. So I told her that I would be available anytime he went over, provided she reminds me! Everyone was tired, so an early night was needed for us all to get ready for the next day.

Yet again, I woke up early, and Philly was already dressed and in the kitchen, cleaning up. She asked me if she could get me some toast. I said, "Sure, go ahead while I put the coffeepot on." I put Napier outside, out of the way, as she always wanted everyone's attention first thing in the morning, and she did it by jumping up to show how much she loved them all.

Everyone had their breakfast and coffee, followed by a walk on the beach; then it was home for a cup of tea at midmorning. George was getting into his cart and motioning to me to come over. When I got there, he asked if I could pick up his trash bag by the door. We loaded the golf cart with the garbage from both houses and then went down to the dock to go to Englewood for our haircuts. I had no idea we would also be visiting the hardware store as well as Publix for jugs of refillable filtered water and other supplies, so it was four hours before we were back at the marina; it looked like a late nap for me that day.

In addition to George's shopping, I was able to shop for Nikki's Christmas present, her favorite bottle of French perfume, along with an appropriate card. At Kmart (next to Publix) was a sale on artificial trees, and it was a great opportunity to buy the tree with a couple of strands of lights and silver garlands. Thank goodness George's cart was at the dock to transport the Christmas tree up to the beach house.

After we unpacked the tree, we realized we had no ornaments, so there were suggestions aplenty of using shells from the beach, some of them even with timeworn holes in them, along with sand dollars. Our task the next day was to dress the tree island style, but now it was time to feed the dog and get washed and dressed for our daily ritual of watching the sun slowly disappear into the Gulf of Mexico. George was probably lying on his couch, reading, as he did when he wanted a quiet evening; you could see him from the beach through the glass sliding door.

We all stood on the white sand, looking for dolphins, pelicans diving, and other seabirds feeding on schools of small fish. Another day was over, with many chores accomplished. Philly organized an evening of playing Country County again to pass the time, and then we were both physically tired and mentally fatigued after being made to play a game where you actually had to use your brain. Then it was one last walk for all of us to the dock to see if there were any fish jumping or any more boats coming in. All of us were then really looking forward to a good night's sleep.

Jeanette said as we were walking back to the house, "How could anyone be so tired by doing practically nothing all day?"

The next six days went by quickly, and Christmas morning was there. Everyone had their coffee and breakfast before opening presents. We all had a lot of fun opening the small gifts. Nikki, Philly, and Jeanette were getting the Christmas turkey plus the fixings all worked out, and the boys were in charge of peeling potatoes, carrots, parsnips, and sprouts. It was a group involvement with the smell of turkey roasting in the oven, which was so pleasing to the senses. I went over to invite George for Christmas dinner, but he said that he had already accepted a previous invitation, but he did add that he would like some leftovers for the next day. Leftovers are always such a tasty meal.

Everyone ate way too much; even the dog had a Christmas plate. We lounged the day away on the porch while Nikki called Julliet and Jonathan, wishing them a merry Christmas in the UK along with cousins and friends. Philly, Jim, and Jeanette called their loved ones also living in England or Scotland.

We all managed a long walk on the beach in the afternoon then went back to the house for another early night after an exhausting Christmas Day. The next few days passed with similar speed, and Nikki's aunt was getting packed to go back home to Burwell, England. Nikki, Jim, and Jeanette all said good-bye to Philly, and I left with her to get on the water taxi to Eldred's Marina.

On the drive to Tampa Airport, Philly was saying she couldn't believe Nikki was enjoying being stuck on the island and not leaving it for weeks at a stretch. I said to her that we had both found a unique place where we could search our inner souls without interference from modern-day interruptions, except for the occasional ring of the telephone. I was amazed as well to know that Nikki was possibly thinking about staying for an extra month.

The trip to the airport went fairly fast, with me trying to convey to a lady who loved her independent lifestyle that island living was good for us. Anyone that had known Aunt Philly for a long time knew that she tired of anything monotonous and would get easily bored. After dropping her off at the Delta check-in curbside and saying good-bye with a "See you in the summer. I hope you are able to sleep your way over the pond," I started the drive back.

Time seemed to drag by, except for the beautiful Skyway Bridge area with its awesome surrounding view of Tampa Bay and the Gulf of Mexico. It certainly wasn't passing as quickly as going, with Philly espousing her philosophical views of life in general, not just to be quarrelsome but to get a quantitative response from any subject she brought up. Her husband Bert, whom I thought a lot of, was not a man of idle chitchat, which probably made their marriage a bit tumultuous, to say the least. I think most of us have someone like that in the family.

Now I wanted to get back to the marina and LGI, and thankfully, Sam was there waiting for me again. He asked, "Well, did you have a nice trip, dropping the auntie off?"

"Sam," I said, "let's say it is going to be a little quieter in the evenings, with a few less thinking games to keep Nikki up past nine."

As always, it was great to see Nikki and Napier waiting for me on the dock. We were both looking forward to sitting on the porch with Jim and Jeanette—just the four of us relaxing with a glass of Cabernet for me and the McGills and Chardonnay for Nikki. She thanked me for taking her aunt to catch her flight, and it felt great being served my dinner with appreciation!

Now we were planning for New Year's Eve. There were so many parties on the island we were invited to, but we really wanted to be with our newfound friends on Peacock Lane. The biggest party was to be held at Bob Pelfrey's golf cart garage in back of his house, with a bonfire and fireworks. It was an open invitation for everyone, and it was where most of the islanders went to be with old acquaintances to bring in the new year. It was very fitting when you think of the Robbie Burns song "Auld Lang Syne." However, the four of us decided to have a small casual party on the front porch. We could still drop by Dick and Doris's around five and a few other places, including the Pelfreys', as long as we were back by seven to call the children in Great Britain along with friends. The Sassers were having their annual oysters on the Bay in the late afternoon, with one having to shuck to have them raw or put on the grill to steam.

It was hard to wait up to see the new year in, so we celebrated at seven when it was the new year in the UK. We all called relatives and friends alike to wish them Happy Hogmanay in Scotland and Happy New Year in England. We were all feeling mellow and happy. There were people dropping by to see us or on the way to the beach where there were a few bonfires at the end of some of the lanes where people were standing around, enjoying fireworks from Boca Grande or setting off their own. We woke up the next morning with a drunken Scotsman on our beach, playing the bagpipes! The year 1996 was officially here.

Jim and Jeanette were getting packed to head home the next day. Lee and Jimetta were going to pick them up at Eldred's Marina. On the last night of their stay, we cooked steaks on the grill, and the McGills told us that they had been pleasantly surprised how much they had enjoyed being on an isolated island. We walked to the beach after supper for one last time and stopped by George's to say good-bye to him; they said that they hoped to be back next year if they were invited! It was another early night as there was a long journey for them the next day.

Breakfast was at the crack of dawn, and then Jim and Jeanette went to walk on the beach by themselves for a final time. When they got back, June was there for them to use her cart to take their luggage to the dock. She had her dogs with her on the cart and drove the luggage down, ready for the water taxi, while the rest of us walked the white, sandy lane. The taxi was on time, and after we all said emotional good-byes, our two Scottish friends floated away from dock 88.

All of us waved and yelled, "See you next year either over here or in Scotland later this year!" We watched while they faded away the closer they got to the marina.

Oh well, it was going to be quiet for a few days before John and Susan Wade came from Cartersville, Georgia, with their white cairn terrier Henry. Back at the house, there was a message on the answering machine from Philly saying she was back home.

"A little tired, but thank you for a lovely stay, and to Lloyd for taking me to the airport." She said that Delta Airlines took good care of her with an extra pillow, so she slept comfortably and that she would call us later after the jet lag diminished.

Treasures

Dock 88

Peacock Lane

Peacock Lane through the Canopy of Trees

Coming into Eldred's Marina by boat

Sunset on the Beach

George's Little Round House

Jim McGill at Eldred's fish weighing station

fishing from our dock

Friends on George's deck at sunset

George on a cool evening

Napier's ride home

George, Lloyd and Napier on the way to the dock

Gathering at George's

Sun Rise on Gasparilla Bay

Casting for Mullet at Sunrise

CHAPTER ELEVEN

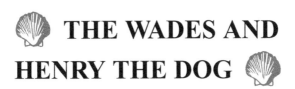 THE WADES AND
HENRY THE DOG

W E WERE LOOKING forward to the next few days of taking it easy, just combing the beach, doing a little fishing, a lot of reading, and a few crossword puzzles. Susan called to say they had booked the water taxi to go to LGI in two days' time for a 3:00 p.m. departure to dock 88 and asked Nikki if that was going to be convenient.

Nikki said, "That is fantastic, Susan! Please give us a call when you get to Englewood as we may need you to shop for a few supplies."

The two days went quickly, starting with a phone call from Jim and Jeanette, saying they got home with no problem except the temperature in Scotland was "bloody freezing." Nikki was on the phone with Jeanette for almost an hour, who talked about her fondness for the island with all its quiet surroundings and just a little love for Napier.

The morning the Wades were to arrive, we cleaned house, made beds, and tried to make the house presentable. Susan duly called to say they were in Englewood and at the Merchant Square Publix, and that if Nikki could give her a list of needs, she and John would gladly pick them up. This would save us a double taxi fare and, more importantly, time off the island.

We headed to the dock to await their arrival at a little past three. The timing couldn't have been better; as we walked up the walkway, we saw that they were almost there and waving as they got closer to pulling alongside where we were standing.

Susan spoke out in her very Southern drawl, "Hey, y'all!" And of course, like all dogs, Henry was first to leap off the boat. He was as white as snow; one could tell that it was not long since he had been at the dog groomers. While we were busy greeting one another, Henry chased Napier, who was ten times larger than him but not as fast. At the beginning of the walkway, there was a small area where they could get into the shallow Bay. Napier waded in with Henry close behind. Needless to say, Henry was immediately rolled over by Napier in all the muddy water.

Susan said, "You can't take that dog anywhere!"

And John said, "Well, at least he was clean for a day or two."

Walking up to the house, John, like our last visitors, wanted to know how we discovered the island. We said that we would tell them at cocktail time, when we could all sit down for the full story. They both stopped on the porch to look at the waves crashing in, and Susan said, "My word, what a sight!"

John nodded his head in agreement and said with a chuckle, "How long can I stay?"

When they looked inside, Susan made a noise like, "Uh-huh, this is basic."

Nikki giggled, saying that she agreed but that it grew on you. John's quick retort was "If you stay too long in one place, it might!"

While Susan unpacked, John made the drinks, with her saying, "I don't care if it's not five o'clock yet. We are now by the sea and officially on our vacation."

John replied, "I think I'll have a drink with you, and we might as well take them on the beach."

Both Nikki and I chimed in to say that there were no rules whatsoever about drinks on the beach—or dogs, for that matter.

We let them go by themselves so that they could take it all in, and they decided to take both dogs with them for a walk. We joined them down there at five to find Napier wet and covered in sand from the churning tide. The clouds were rolling in, and it looked like a cold front might be coming, making the waves higher than normal.

John said, "I believe I'll walk back for a fresh beer," with Nikki saying, "We'll be close behind you."

We fed the two dogs and started the charcoal in the barbecue. We were having ribs as our main course that night, and there was still time to watch the sunset while drinks were refreshed and giving the charcoal a chance to burn down. The ribs were finger-licking good, and after dinner, we all walked to the dock to show our guests the lights on the causeway to Boca Grande. You could see the white sandy lane in the dark of the night to guide your travels.

Back home, we all sat on the porch, in the swing, or on the white plastic chairs. Our conversation was about all our mutual friends on Lake Nottely and, of course, our children. The Wades were weary from traveling most of the day and went off for a much-needed sleep at about 9:00 p.m. We were not too far behind them.

I woke up at about 3:00 a.m. with the sound of John opening his bedroom door and going to the bathroom. Napier left our room to see what was going on and noticed that the Wades' bedroom door was open and the bed was empty. That was too good to pass up, so the huge dog climbed into John's bed, sand and all! John found his way back into the room in the dark and got into bed. As he lay down, he found Napier next to him in the small single bed. John shouted, "Damn dog!"

We heard John shaking the sandy sheet, and Napier then went over to Susan's bed to sniff out Henry, who was in bed with her.

After a few slaps to Napier's nose under her sheet, we heard Susan say, "No, Napier, no!"

John finally got Napier out of the room. We went back to sleep, laughing in a very low giggle because you could hear everything through the thin walls.

We all woke up fairly early; the cold front seemed to have passed through, and the morning looked promising. I poured myself a mug of coffee and found John on the porch drinking his. When I asked him about Napier visiting him and Susan during the night, he chuckled and said, "What a shock to find a huge hairy, sandy dog in my bed."

Susan appeared, saying, "Trust John not to close our bedroom door. Napier only wanted a soft bed to lie on instead of a hard floor."

The rest of the day was spent walking on the beach and sitting on the dock, reading or taking a nap. John said to me, "After a week of this kind of life, one could get really lazy. How long have you been here?"

He couldn't believe it when I said, "About six weeks."

Soon it was time to get ready for a sunset get-together on George's deck, the first for John and Susan. We could see the others arriving with snacks and their favorite beverages, so the four of us walked quickly over with our offerings as they were waving for us to hurry up because the sun was going down.

Nikki introduced our guests to the gang who either had a place on Peacock Lane or lived close by. After all the introductions, we all got into the island way, with the guys talking about fishing while the girls discussed their treasures of sharks' teeth, seashells, and sand dollars that they had found that day.

We all dispersed after sunset, and as we were doing so, Louise asked us down to their house the following morning for breakfast about nine. We all said, "Yes, that would be lovely. We'll see you tomorrow." After a coffee or tea on the porch before turning in, we asked the Wades if they were going to keep their bedroom door closed. Susan replied, "Yes, if a certain man can remember what happened last night."

I woke to put the dog out and again found John on the porch, drinking coffee. He said for me to grab myself a cup. We didn't say much while we were drinking and watching Napier and Henry sniffing around the trees. We occasionally glanced at the shore to see the pelicans in formation, flying low, skimming the water. We then took the girls coffee to remind them about our breakfast date on the Bay with the Sassers.

We strolled down the lane to their house on the left, which was surrounded by scrub oaks and coconut palms. Their dog came out to greet us, and Louise told the Wades that his name was Snook and really belonged to their son Robert back in Wauchula. "Even though Snook spends most of his time on our porch back home."

All the dogs played well together, and we sat down on benches beside a long trestle table on their front porch overlooking the Bay. Louise brought out homemade biscuits, scrambled eggs, bacon, grits, and sausage patties along with tomato gravy—enough food to feed an army. Being Southerners (except for Nikki), we couldn't wait to dig in. Nikki never did acquire a taste for tomato gravy or grits, but it was a scrumptious breakfast!

While digesting our food with Louise's homemade sweet tea (another Southern thing Nikki couldn't get used to), we were enjoying watching the boats coming and going. Nikki said that she hadn't seen Bob and June recently. Ed went on to tell us that they were away, going to the University of Florida Gators football games. Ed said that now that they had finished with the Sugar Bowl in New Orleans, they would be back to the island within the next few weeks. He asked John where he hailed from, and John replied, "Cartersville, just north of Atlanta, with a house on Lake Nottely near Blairsville on the North Carolina state line."

"We both have cousins in that area," Ed piped in and mentioned that they had visited them in the past in order to get away from the Florida heat.

After helping Louise to clear up, we all went for a walk on the beach with the three dogs in tow. We looked for sharks' teeth while the dogs were chasing sandpipers, optimistic that they would catch one—which, of course, would never happen. We started to walk north toward the park to show the Wades how beautiful it was, and Ranger Rick happened to be on duty. He was also married to an English girl from the London area, and we passed the time of day with him before walking back to Peacock Lane.

John wanted to go fishing in the surf; he said, "Do you have any bait, Lloyd?" I said that we could catch sand fleas, which are really very small crabs barely under the sand when the water recedes. The whiting would take the bait since that is what they mostly feed on. We fished for over an hour, catching enough for supper and maybe lunch the following day. Jerry Ridings walked down while we were there to say that we had more company than anyone else he knew. He told me that if our guests wanted to come back next winter, we could use his house for the overflow, as he hardly ever used the house from November through March (it's too cold for Floridians in the winter).

We walked back with Jerry to clean the fish at the cleaning station on our dock. George drove his cart down, bringing a couple of filleting knives. We invited George over for the fish supper, but he suggested bringing them over to his house to cook them as he had lots of fish coating. John asked if we were feeding the multitude, and George said he could as he had some frozen grouper that he could add to the feast. That was to be another fish-fry dinner party, and word got around on the Lane. All the ladies would bring the side dishes.

I went back to shower, have lunch, and take a brief nap. Susan was reading, and Nikki was doing her crossword. She had finished another murder mystery book, which most likely would have been an Agatha Christie novel. Nikki suggested that, after the guys had their nap, we could all go to the library to exchange our books. Nikki volunteered to walk to June's to let her know about the dinner party at George's while we were resting.

Arriving at the library, Susan was surprised to see such a variety on the shelves (not only ones for adults, but children's books also), and there were lots to choose from. You hardly see children on LGI in the winter, but I understood that in the summer, it was a different story, with Floridians from inland flocking to the cooler sea breezes by the water. We were walking on the beach again, still amazed that it was so empty, and then, out of the blue, we met a lady whom Nikki knew a little. Her name was Laura, and she always walked in her bathing suit. She was very tanned and soft-spoken, with a Southern drawl. Her husband was a self-employed man who worked mostly on LGI as a carpenter, and they lived on the south end of the island. Laura walked most days the entire length of the beach, stopping often to pick up shells, which resulted in her having an enviable collection.

Back at the beach house, it was time to get ready for the fish fry at sunset. John said that they had to go to the Sebring racetrack the next day to see his son, who was racing there in the twelve-hour endurance race, so we called the Eldred's taxi for a 10:00 a.m. pickup on the dock. We all got showered and dressed and set off to George's round house for the sunset gathering. Everyone showed up with pots and trays of fixings, mainly Southern-type sides that go with fried fish such as hush puppies, grits, and baked beans. For dessert, there was a large pan of pineapple upside-down cake. Nikki and Louise were helping George fry the fish as the guys were talking about most of the fish being caught only that morning. The favorite fish, of course, was the grouper—a thick, flaky white meat that was absolutely delicious! We were all enjoying the wonderful food while watching the sun go down in the blue Gulf waters.

Everyone was making their way back home, saying to the Wades, "See you next year!" We walked with June back to her large home, taking Napier and Henry with us, and carried on down the lane to see what was happening on the Bay. The Sassers, since they lived on the Bay, also walked with us, so there were five dogs in total being walked, and they were all enjoying the social activity. We got back home tired, and after saying good night to John and Susan, we all went to bed.

In the morning, we woke to see our guests getting ready for their departure from LGI. After breakfast, they had a last walk on the beach, and then we all left for the dock. Susan said how the island was a true treasure and "Where else could you lose yourself in time?" They couldn't thank us enough for the experience and were looking forward to seeing us back in Blairsville in early spring. Sam was right on time and ready to take them back to Eldred's Marina where their car was parked. Waving from the boat, Susan yelled, "Thanks again, y'all!" in her lovely Georgia accent.

Walking back toward the house, Nikki reminded me that Jacque and David were coming near the end of February as they wanted to escape part of the English winter. I said it would be great having them to stay and see what they thought about the island. It was always fun getting people's reactions. I would get the hammock up for David, where he could read or fall asleep in the warm afternoons. She said that after the Bevans got there, the Andersons, Daniels, and Boyettes would like to rent a cottage for a week during their stay as they were all old friends. We decided we would ask Tommy and Amber if it would be okay to extend our time there until the end of March. We had discussed it in the past few weeks, with Nikki being a little hesitant at first, worried about getting back to work our antique shop.

"Hurray!" I said. "That would be awesome, my darling, as you know I love this place and want to stay as long as possible."

Then it was back to reality when Nikki said, "We both have to go to the antiques fair at Newark on Trent and the Swinderby mammoth fair in early February so that our antiques can arrive in Blue Ridge in early April, to start the summer sales season."

Julliet would fly over to stay with Napier while we were in England. Jonathan would try to join us and help if he could get away from his studies, but of course, we couldn't bank on it! It would, however, be a bonus to see him while in England. Our client John in Tampa might need another shipment, and if he did, that would help pay our expenses to the UK. I asked Nikki if she wanted to go on Delta in business elite as we had enough miles to upgrade.

"Fantastic," she said. "It's so nice to be wined and dined across the Atlantic."

We decided that on the way back, we could stay with Gillian and David just outside the Gatwick Airport area in Three Bridges.

We secured the airline tickets that day and called Paul and Lorraine at the Brownlow Arms in Hough on the Hill to secure our room for seven nights. Nikki thought that we should build in an extra two days so that we could stay with the Bevans on the last Sunday at the end of the trip. And she also suggested that we get Mick to pack our containers at the show to give us more time to buy. That would result in extra earnings, which would more than cover the cost of having someone else doing the packing. It made sense because, as we bought, it became easier to judge how much more we had to buy to finish off the huge forty-foot-high cube container. With that agreed, we realized that we had quite a bit to do, including sending about fifty thousand dollars to the bank that worked with us (by giving a commercial exchange rate with lower transfer fees).

For the first time in weeks, we were by ourselves. We both loved to have company, but we also loved our solitude. The rest of the day was for lounging around, only interrupted by walking on the beach with the dog. Later, George called me over and wanted to throw the cast net off the dock to catch mullet. The mullet were always around somebody's dock, and most of us on Peacock Lane loved fried mullet. We netted enough for supper, and while filleting them, George said that he would do the cooking if we brought the coleslaw over.

It was a nice way of life that cost very little, just some effort and time. While we were at the dock, Nikki got a call from Lynn and Barry Varian, our friends from the North Georgia mountains, to say that they were on their way to visit us with Maggie, their dog. Maggie was a sort of hero on Lake Nottely, after chasing off two Chow dogs when they tried to pin her on the ground. Maggie was victorious in the short fight. One of the Chows came very close to biting my leg on a previous encounter when I was walking Napier. Our guests would be on the island later that afternoon, as they had booked the Pirates' taxi for four o'clock. Napier and I would be able to get a nap in, and then I'd call Barry on his cell phone for some last-minute shopping if they got to Englewood early. Nikki suggested they get a rotisserie chicken along with a couple of sides from the grocery store in the middle of town. After forty winks, I helped Nikki clean the house by sweeping the porch, along with washing the windows inside. It seemed to us that blowing sand reached areas of more than two hundred feet from the beach.

Then it was time to walk down the lane with Napier to wait for the new arrivals. As they pulled up to the dock, Maggie jumped off the boat; she was glad to see Napier again, and we were likewise glad to see our friends. They had their luggage and lots of groceries—enough for all of us to take a bag or two each up to the house. Lynn was a little taken aback at how the beach house looked. We said that we didn't think about it like that, that we just thought how fortunate we were to be there all winter.

LLOYD ARTHUR WIGGINS AND ROSEMARY EGERTON LETTS

We made our drinks and trotted over to George's for sunset, and George was pleased to be in the company of two gorgeous ladies. Those old blue eyes sparkled when he talked to Nikki and Lynn. Maggie and Napier were chasing birds on the beach and having lots of fun despite having no success. They both loved playing in the surf and lying on the cool sand, while we all talked and waited for the sun to disappear into the horizon. We went back to the house to have supper and then retreated to the porch, where we talked until it was time to go to bed. Nikki wanted to have all the gossip from Lynn's trips as a flight attendant and the friends and neighbors we shared on Lake Nottely. Lynne was a volunteer with different charities and on the board of the Humane Society along with the Lake Nottely Association in Blairsville, so there were lots to talk about.

We were finally off to bed so that we could show our friends the island in the morning. We could hear Lynn in the bathroom, and she was not happy with the smelly brown water coming out of the shower. Lynn, being a flight attendant for Delta for the past twenty-five years, and Barry, running his side of a large business in London, England, were used to a little better accommodation. Barry called out to her and asked if everything was all right.

"Not exactly," she replied. "The water in here is disgusting!"

After that calamity, we all settled in for some sleep.

The next morning came quickly, with Barry, myself, and Napier waking up first. While the girls were still sleeping, we took our coffee to the dock, with Napier leading the way, to watch the sun rise. After about three-quarters of an hour, the sun rose to spray light all over the Bay. It was an amazing sight, and Barry was very impressed. He said Lynn would want her coffee by then, and I said that Nikki would be the same. She didn't seem to function well without her caffeine first thing every morning. When we got back to the house, the girls were finally up, with Barry in charge of making a pot of fresh coffee to go with toast and waffles.

Lynn asked how we could stand such inconveniences such as the lack of clean running water or a bathtub with its plughole eaten out with rust. We both said such trivial things were worth putting up with just to be in a place like this. I think she was used to better-equipped places to visit in the swanky areas of the Florida Panhandle or Boca Raton during the summer and fall. The Panhandle was pretty darn cold during that time of year, being three hundred miles north; it makes a big difference when the cold fronts come through. Anyway, we loved the place, and yes, it would be nice to be living in a luxury house or condo, but at that time in our lives, we couldn't afford it.

The Varians asked how the antique business was going, and we told them it was going very well even though it was on borrowed money. We used our house as collateral for the buying trips to England, so to spend thousands of dollars on winter vacations wouldn't make sense. One day, we felt we would be able to afford a better place to use, but not right then while we were building up our inventory in the antique warehouse.

After breakfast, we all walked to the south end of the island, with the dogs playing in the surf and chasing sandpipers. Buddy Gaines's dog, Sophie, came out to meet Maggie, and they all played well together. We had a lazy day walking, reading and sitting on the porch in the shade, and greeting a few of the residents on Peacock Lane.

It was getting close to five o'clock, and Nikki was inside, getting ready, making snacks for the gathering with George when Julliet came up the steps, surprising us with an early visit. Nikki was tearfully overwhelmed, reaching out to hug our daughter. Lynn said that she wished Megan would give her a surprise visit sometime, and as Julliet moved aside to embrace her mother, Lynn could see her daughter Megan right behind her—she had traveled down with Julliet! Now Lynn, Nikki, Julliet, and Megan were all crying, with Barry amazingly saying, "When I show up, no one cries."

At that moment, everyone laughed!

At that rate, we were going to be late getting to George's. Julliet said she flew into Charlotte so that she could travel to Boone to see friends, and that was where she and Megan cooked up a plan to visit their mothers—since they were together on a secluded island that no one had ever heard of. So they had driven through the night to get there before Lynn and Barry were due to leave in a day's time.

Nikki could not wait to introduce her daughter to our new friends that evening, especially June and George. We were all in the mood to have a celebration. You could see it in Nikki's face how happy she was to have her daughter with her again, since she'd been at university these past three years. June and George, after learning that Julliet was staying on the island to look after Napier for the next two weeks while we travelled to the UK to work, told her that if she needed anything, such as a ride to the mainland to go shopping or help in any way, to just call or knock on their door. We were relieved to know that Julliet would not be alone because our friends would be there for her. A sense of well-being came over us, knowing we could put our worries aside.

We all went back to our house to cook out on the barbecue and socialize as if we were still in the mountains. Then it was a walk to the beach for the six of us and the two dogs. I went to bed, while Nikki and Lynn and their daughters sat on the porch, going over what had been going on for the past few years.

The next morning came quickly, and the girls were getting up while Barry and I had coffee, fed the dogs, walked them, and sat on the dock again to get out of the girls' way while they all got up and dressed. He said they were leaving that day to drive to his daughter's winter home on the beach in a modern new village called Seaside, close to Destin on the Panhandle of Northwest Florida. Nikki and I went with them last year for a week's holiday, driving down from Lake Nottely in Lynn's Jeep. That gave us a chance to visit other friends who were customers of ours living close by in Watercolor, and the Lovejoys at their antique shop on Panama City Beach, where they sold a mixture of Old World antiquities as well as modern-day decorative items.

By the time we got back to the house, with the dogs behind us, Nikki was making a breakfast of coffee and toast. Lynn asked Barry what time they should call for the water taxi, remembering that it would take approximately seven hours to drive to their destination. After some discussion, they decided they could be ready for pickup at noon. Megan said she would go up with them and fly back to Boone, North Carolina, via either Charlotte or Asheville. I think Lynn was looking forward to clean running water to shower in, not to mention a bed larger than a three-foot bunk.

After breakfast and a short walk on the beach, it was time to get the luggage—along with Lynn, Barry, Megan, and Maggie—down to the dock, and then we saw them off, waving as they disappeared in the distance, going across Gasparilla Bay through the channel and under the overhanging trees going into the marina. We were now getting excited because, in a few days, we would be on our way to London to buy antiques for our warehouse in Blue Ridge, Georgia.

The rest of the day, Nikki and Julliet were either walking the beach, Julliet being shown around the island, or just spending time as a mother and daughter. On one of their walks on the beach, Julliet brought a coconut back with her and asked me if I could open it. After handing it to me, I shook it to see if there was still milk in it; the coconut was dry and would not be safe or good to eat. We then walked down the lane where there were lots of them lying under the palm trees. We both shook a few to find one with lots of milk and took them back to the house to chop them open; but first, we went over to George's to borrow an axe. It was hard work, chopping down on an oblong object that kept escaping through the front yard.

I could see George looking over and smiling, probably bringing back memories of him doing the same thing for his children. We finally managed it, with all of us having a taste of the deliciously fresh coconut. So far, Julliet loved the island, with its pristine white sandy beaches, the smell of seaweed, and the salt air fragrances penetrating her senses, helping her asthma. The day went by quite fast; it was time to get washed, dressed in our beachy evening attire, and then off to George's deck.

He welcomed us onto the deck, asking if there was anything new to report. Nikki said, "We are off tomorrow to London for two weeks, George. We are going to miss you and Julliet and the island, of course. We told Julliet that she would be in good hands since you know all the foibles of this place."

He said, "I will certainly take you over to Eldred's to either get your car or take the taxi to the airport."

We said, "Thank you very much," and accepted the offer. After sunset, we told him, "See you in the morning, George, have a good night."

At the house, I cooked hamburgers on the grill while the girls made salad. It was time for me to go to bed while they stayed up, still talking about Julliet's life at university. I heard Nikki coming to bed a couple of hours later when she whispered softly, "Good night, darling."

CHAPTER TWELVE

🐚 COMMUTING TO BRITAIN WITH NIKKI 🐚

AFTER SAYING GOOD-BYE to Julliet and thanking George again for taking us to Eldred's, Nikki and I got a taxi from the marina to Tampa Airport for the 2:00 p.m. flight connecting with the 5:30 red-eye to London, arriving at Gatwick the next morning. We were looking forward to going business class all the way, flying through the night and getting to England at 11:00 a.m. GMT (6:00 a.m., Tampa time). It usually took us a couple of days to adjust to British time, and I decided I would get to bed as soon as we got to a hotel. Nikki always stayed up all day, fighting the jet lag; she was a lot tougher than I was! I found it easier to give in rather than fight it.

The flight to Atlanta in the first-class section was very comfortable and seemed to go quickly since we talked all the way about our expectations for the next two weeks. After arriving, we went to check into the business elite lounge on concourse E. It had a very long bar with an equally long buffet station; after ordering our drinks and having a tasty snack, Nikki said, "I will see you at the gate as I am going to the duty-free shop to buy perfume for Jacque."

I could see Nikki coming down the corridor from my seat, just outside the gate. Her smile was very attractive, and her hair was bouncy, as it always was, while she walked. Of course, she had never noticed any such trivial details about herself.

We were called to preboard the airplane almost immediately, a large jumbo jet with two huge engines under its wings, with another sitting on the fuselage in the tail. We were both welcomed aboard with a "Nice to see you again, Mr. and Mrs. Wiggins" as we were escorted to our seats, which were large, soft leather armchairs connected in pairs throughout first-class section. The flight attendant was one we had flown with before and recognized us as friends of Lynn Varian, who also worked the London Gatwick flight once a week. Our flight attendant, being very tall and thin with very curly hair, was easily recognizable. She had also attended a few parties at Lynn and Barry's house on Lake Nottely along with other Delta flight attendants who flew routes to London or other European cities. She asked us if we would like an orange juice, mimosa, or champagne.

Nikki replied, "We both will have champagne, and now that we are officially seated, Wilma, please call us Lloyd and Nikki."

The flight was smooth, with hardly any turbulence. Nikki ordered the full five-course meal while I ordered off the express menu, hoping to get some sleep. After a couple of hours, I woke up and I looked over at Nikki to see her enjoying the cheese, crackers, and fruit with a large Chardonnay. She woke me up over Ireland, saying they were serving breakfast then and we should be landing in just over an hour. When I heard that, I hugged my extra pillow harder with delight. I was scrunched up against the window and had had a pretty good sleep. I asked her to order me the cooked breakfast with a cup of tea, if she would please, while I get a few more minutes of sleep. While departing the aircraft, we said thank you and good-bye to our flight attendant and told her that we'd see her on the next trip or at Lynn's house that summer.

We hurried down the hallways at Gatwick and through immigration to take our luggage, two heavy suitcases, off the fast-moving carousel. Nikki bought our train tickets after the long queue moved quickly with so many tellers selling tickets. It really didn't matter since there were trains to our destination leaving every twenty minutes, and we had all day to get to Hough on the Hill in Lincolnshire.

From the teller's instruction at the station inside the main terminal building, we found platform 4 down the escalator for the Thameslink train that went across London to King's Cross to connect to our north-running train. We started to read the station signs after crossing the river Thames. When we got to Blackfriars Bridge Station, Nikki said it was only a few more stops. We finally got to King's Cross and dragged our luggage up high concrete stairs to the street level, and then there was a ten-minute walk through the streets to the main train terminal. Thank goodness at the end of our trip we could put all our winter gear in the container going to the antique shop in Georgia so that we wouldn't have to drag extra suitcases back across London.

After a short wait, we were on our way to Newark on Trent after paying for a SuperSaver return ticket of fifty pounds each. While on the train, we decided to go to the first-class dining car for a light breakfast. Soon after that, we got to Newark on Trent Station, and then it was only a five-minute walk to pick up the panel van at Falcon Motors. Nikki said that she would wait with the luggage if I went and paid for the van. She said that she would also call Jonathan in Scotland from the station. After loading up, we were in the van and excited to finally be there; after a loving kiss, we were on our way. Nikki suggested that after a couple of hours' sleep, we could go into Grantham to shop for antiques.

We got to Hough on the Hill and an ancient inn known as the Brownlow Arms, famous locally for its gourmet meals. The hotel was run by owners/operators Paul and Lorraine Willoughby, with the help of Paul's dad, Les, and their friend Beryl. They took care of all their guests' needs very well. We quietly slipped through the unlocked large oak door to hear Lorraine tell Beryl that she hoped Pierre was later than normal as his room was not ready. I said in a French accent, "'Elloou, 'elloou, Lorraine!"

She spun around, saying, "Christ! Pierre is here." When she came out and saw us instead, she said, "Lloyd, I'm going to get even with you for giving me such a fright."

After hugs and kisses, Beryl indicated that she thought it was pretty funny to scare them about Pierre being early, and I announced that I was going to take a two-hour nap before going out to buy antiques with my beautiful wife Nikki.

Nikki said, "Hush, and take the luggage to our room and have your nap."

We took our van to the center of Grantham in the early afternoon, where the antique shops were located. We bought lots of old leather-bound books and as many small antique items and decorative ware as we could—if they were a good price, of course. These little pieces could be placed in corners of the container, so they virtually went free. We always tried to buy lots of plates, paintings, mirrors, brass or copper fireplace boxes, shovels, forks, and pokers. Flow blue china dinner services were the most popular for the dealers to buy from us wholesale when a shipment first arrived at our warehouse in Georgia.

We were then off to the antique warehouse in Newark on Trent, where we would see Claire, Bill Pedley, and Nick, the owner. These three have always been very welcoming, not only to us but to our buyers whom we courier for. We always socialized with Claire and her very nice farmer friend Will Sergeant of Stragglethorpe either at the Brownlow Arms or at their house. Claire was a fantastic cook who made her pies from homegrown fruit, and they were delicious! The antique warehouse specialized in Georgian furniture, which was usually too highly priced for us, but still worth a look, as sometimes they had a sleeper, as they say in the trade—which means something that was not rated by its vendor. We had bought a bit of flow blue from them, and Claire invited us for dinner on Friday night. Nikki said we would gladly come if they would be our guest at the Brownlow (known for their home-cooked cuisine, such as Lincolnshire sausages, lamb shank, and a variety of other local dishes) the following Tuesday evening.

We often had to pass through Stragglethorpe on our way to Hough on the Hill after a day of working the shows. Stragglethorpe is made up of Will's farm, a twelfth-century church, and a few cottages. Whenever we saw Will on his tractor or at the barns, we would stop to have a chat, and he would say, "Now then, Lloyd, how is everything going? Nice to see you again," in his broad Lincolnshire brogue.

We went back to the Brownlow Arms for a shower, then went down to the bar area to relax; we would have the place to ourselves, with no other guests, since they were closed on Sundays. When we arrived, Paul and Lorraine were calling in for a Chinese takeaway and asked us if we wanted to order as well. We agreed and asked him to let us know how much it was. We went upstairs to get ready, and we could hear Pierre in the next room with his wife, also called Lorraine. The small inn had seven bedrooms, and since it was fully booked, there should be others who were staying there attending the massive antique fairs. There were probably some from the States that we might know.

We went down to the lounge, which had a look like something out of an Emily Brontë novel—a coal-burning fireplace, settees, and overstuffed armchairs throughout. A note was at the bar for us to serve ourselves; we just had to jot down what we had on the honor system. Pierre and Lorraine walked into the lounge, very pleased to see us. He asked if Paul had left to go to Grantham for the Chinese takeaway, and no sooner had he got the question out when Paul walked in with plenty of extra rations for everyone.

Pierre was thankful that they wouldn't have to go out to find a place to eat on a Sunday, when most restaurants were closed. We all traipsed out to the dining room for a buffet of small Chinese pagoda-looking white boxes full of tasty food. We helped ourselves, taking samples of everything that was offered, eating while talking about what we'd been doing for the past six months since we'd last seen one another during the August fairs. It was great to be back with some of our antiques friends.

We asked Paul who else was staying there, and he said probably no one that we knew since they were all British, Dutch, or Irish. Pierre had to leave early to set up his large marquee, shared with a couple of fellow exhibitors. Nikki and I wanted to be out after breakfast around eight thirty the next morning since we would have to line up to get our overseas buyer's passes. The two individual passes cost ninety-five pounds for parking the van inside the set-up area. The rest of the day would be spent buying more antiques.

We woke up the following day to a full English breakfast with pots of tea for me and coffee for Nikki. However, we left the fried bread and black pudding (which is made from the blood of cows). Nikki said, "Hurry up, we have to go to Barclays Bank in Newark for more cash to buy with."

The money had been set up a few weeks before we came over. When we were in the bank, an American was there with American Express traveler's checks that he wanted to exchange for British pounds. They told him that the money had to be ordered since they would never have that amount available without prior notice. He was incensed that a bank would not have cash for traveler's checks to serve tourists and business people. We had also learned that the hard way in the past.

The bank teller took a lot of time counting our money, and then we were on our way to see what we could buy at the mammoth fair just outside of Lincoln. We lined up to go in as overseas buyers. Nikki got out of our van to walk in to get a better view of what was on offer to buy early on vendors' trailers and their estate cars. I asked her to look out for stained glass windows for me as she was looking for garden fountains, urns, and statues.

We had walkie-talkies to keep in contact, and we gave one to Mick, our container packer, and his porters.

The place was wild! You saw buyers from America, Italy, Russia, and the Orient with satchels, man bags, or trousers with many pockets stuffed with cash to purchase millions of dollars' worth of antiques. One could spend ten pounds (sterling) on a stained glass window and make more money than on a large armoire (like the one used as a prop in JR's office on *Dallas*, the soap opera) for five thousand English pounds. It would probably be a Louis XV piece of furniture turned into a cloak cupboard or a cocktail cabinet; that was a very trendy piece of furniture at that time, favored by interior designers and decorators.

We had a goal of buying enough furniture to fill a forty-foot container; I did, anyway, since acquiring furniture was my main responsibility, to fill up most of the space. The best-selling items back in Blue Ridge were dark Black Forest carved wood items from Eastern Europe, marble-top furniture, and from Ireland, chicken-cage kitchen dressers with the bottom looking like a plate rack, but it was actually a cage door. Those were to keep chickens in a warm kitchen during cold winters, for eggs and meat. The Irish dealers were the toughest to barter with; Nikki didn't even try, as they could be quite condescending and patronizing at the best of times.

The buying was going great, and I could hear Nikki on the radio calling for a pickup from Mick or one of his workers. We both bought a lot of stuff; we used Eastern European dogcarts to put small items in while letting the boys pick up the furniture along with heavy boxes of china. Nikki called up to meet me at Pierre's marquee for coffee, and more importantly, she needed more money to buy with. Tony, the Nottingham dealer, was in Pierre's tent to greet us, and his wife made us coffee, which helped us warm up.

We had been buying all day, and by 4:00 p.m., Nikki called on her radio; she said it was time to leave. Vendors were closing up because of darkness and the drizzling rain. On our way back to the inn, our priorities were a hot bath with a cup of tea. We were pretty cold, wet, and weary, but still euphoric about the successful buying because the February shows are always risky. The weather dictated if the antique shows would be fully attended by dealers selling their goods, especially in Scotland, Germany, or Eastern Europe where so many of them came from. They would bring huge moving trucks filled with eighteenth- and nineteenth-century furniture along with primitive farm implements like hundreds of handmade pitchforks, hand-carved troughs and dough bowls, and farm wagons large and small.

We were anxious to get downstairs with our notes and to sit by the fire with a glass of wine, telling each other what we had bought. Paul's dad, Les, was the only other person in the lounge, so after kidding around with him pretending to speak Spanish or French, he darted to the kitchen where he was told to peel potatoes.

Nikki couldn't wait to tell me all about her purchases, and after half an hour, Lorraine appeared behind the bar to ask if we found our Cabernet Sauvignon and Chardonnay. We confirmed that we had remembered that Paul always stored it in the fridge behind the counter in the dining room. Nikki asked her what the special was that night on the menu.

"Lamb shank" was the reply.

"That's for me," I said. Nikki was contemplating a very rare steak.

Pierre and his Lorraine came down and said hello to us, also inquiring what the menu special was. We asked Pierre if his day had been a success. He said not bad; however, the other vendors in his marquee sold a lot as well, especially Tony Grimes. Beryl came in to ask us to go into the dining room, where we could sit together and continue talking business. Pierre said he had quite a few turn-of-the-century three- and four-door armoires, like the ones I had bought in the past, back in his warehouse, if I needed any more for the containers. Our Florida customer usually purchased at least five four-door wardrobes for his warehouse and a few bedroom suites with marble tops, as well as sideboards with marble insets.

Nikki said that when we were at Jacque and David's in Hathersage, I could go to Pierre's warehouse and get back by train within six hours. That sounded like a plan, but thinking quietly, only if there was enough money left over after the two antique fairs.

That trip was important for us as we were moving into a much larger warehouse in a couple of months, closer to the center of Blue Ridge, which was a tourist town with a mountain railway train that goes to McCaysville, Tennessee, and back. We said good night to everyone and went off to bed for an early night. We hoped to be out first thing in the morning, about 8:00 a.m., buying antiques by nine and coordinating with Mick to ensure pickups were done the previous day after we had left the showground. In the bedroom, we continued talking about what we had bought, and Nikki was very pleased that the prices were good enough for us to double our investment at a wholesale level, and then it was off to sleep.

We had another full English breakfast that would keep us going for most of the day. The hot dog or sausage stands at the showgrounds were pretty gross, but not as foul as the portaloos, placed strategically around the one-hundred-acre field marked out for at least two thousand vendors and three thousand buyers from around the globe. We arrived at the gates of Swinderby with passes to park again inside (without lining up, this time). After meeting up with our porters at Mick's, we would then drive to Pierre's where we parked the van to use as a staging area, carefully positioning our vehicle so as not to block any of the dealers' paths behind the marquee that they shared with others.

Then we were off buying again with dogcarts that were stored in Bill Pedley's tent overnight. Nikki said to meet her in Pierre's marquee at noon. I told her that would be good as I was going over to the Dutch boys to buy strip-pine furniture if the price was right, and then I'd see her at twelve. Buying was slow as we were covering the same ground as the day before but hoping that the prices were going to be better. When I met up with Nikki, she still had enough money to continue. Later, we stopped for coffee and a warm-up before the final walk-through.

Nikki asked me if I had been by AJ's pitch to see if Gavin had any merchandise that was useful. They were a husband-and-wife team that we had done business with over the years. My reply to her was that I would the next day, when the show was starting to break up. They always had blowout furniture if they decided not to set up at the Newark showground. Both showgrounds were once bomber bases during World War II. The runways of the old airbases were the best place to buy because of the accessibility. The lanes leading off the tarmac were okay if it didn't rain, which made the lanes soft and muddy; the pickup vehicles always got bogged down. What we were buying on that was at the right price because some vendors were leaving early to get out of the wet, cold winter.

Nikki wanted to leave by 4:00 p.m. to have a hot bath and be down in the lounge by five. It would be almost dark by then. Driving back through the Lincolnshire countryside, with its high hedges and small, winding rural roads, Nikki said, "Oh my goodness, Will and Claire are coming for dinner tonight!"

I had forgotten all about us having set up a dinner date. We were both now really looking forward to being with them again.

Back at the inn, we told Lorraine about our guests arriving; they knew Will and Claire very well due to their many visits there. We aimed to be ready for our five o'clock rendezvous in the lounge to reserve four overstuffed chairs beside the fireplace.

Les was sitting on the end barstool with two other friends when we walked in. They were introduced to us, a nice group of guys, kidding me about the last Ryder Cup of golf. Nikki returned with our favorite drinks, and no sooner did we settle down when Lorraine came downstairs with the phone, saying that a frantic Julliet needed to speak to her daddy.

Julliet told me in a panicky voice that there was a snake up in the tree by the porch, and it was devouring another snake. I told her that black or indigo snakes eat poisonous snakes, usually small rattlers, so she was a little relieved. Julliet also said that a suspected northeasterly front was forming off the coast of Southwest Florida. George had already taken Julliet under his wing, so he would know if and when to evacuate. I asked her to keep us up to date with the news, and with that, we said good night.

Will and Claire arrived while we were still in the lounge. Claire commented on how cold and nasty the weather was outside, and it was so nice to be sat in comfy chairs beside a roaring fire. Will said in his Lincolnshire brogue, "Now then, Lloyd, how is the buying going at the antique show?"

"Fantastic," I said. "We think we may have enough for a container." I mentioned that we would need to be very selective at the Newark show and look mainly for small items made of china, ironstone, or carved wood, which seemed to be in demand from decorators in Georgia and North Carolina. Pierre and Lorraine came in, and we introduced everyone, saying that Will and Claire would be joining us for dinner; everyone was delighted. The dinner was superb, and Pierre even tried a cold Cabernet with comments of "Not bad, Lloyd. It does go well with lamb."

After dinner, we adjourned to the lounge for coffee and, once consumed, said good night to everyone. Nikki wanted to go up to get ready for the next fair by counting what money was left to buy with. Mick would let us know by the second day of the fair how much, if any more, furniture would be needed to fill in space. It is always better to have too much by a sideboard or two rather than to be short by the same amount. It was off to sleep quickly so we'd be ready for a 5:00 a.m. wake-up call—too early to have breakfast at the inn, so we would get an egg-and-bacon roll from a vendor at the showgrounds.

It was still dark as we were walking through the gates. We were both full of anticipation. What could we find on the way to pick up our dogcarts? We stopped to see the pieces being displayed beside the tarmac. Mick and the boys were waiting for us, and we all turned on our walkie-talkies. Nikki covered a different area and asked me to meet her at the overseas buyers lounge in two hours' time at 8:30 a.m.

The first two hours were going to be most important to get the best buys before the other antique buyers saw them. We both filled our carts in the first sixty minutes while calling in some larger pieces to the boys at the container, just outside blue gate 1. I could hear Nikki on the radio talking to Mick's son, Paul, to pick up windows at the B and C avenues. Our friends Ed and Anne were set up next to the overseas buyers lounge on three pitches, where they used one for their caravan to sleep, eat, and make tea in. Walking by, I saw that Nikki was having coffee and a cigarette with Anne, so we changed that to our meeting place. Also, she needed more money since the buying was extremely good that day.

Nikki suggested that we meet again at the lounge at noon or, if the money ran out, she would call me to meet up earlier. Getting a little tired, I went to the van parked beside the container for a nap—with my radio on, just in case Nikki called. After that, it was time to meet up at the lounge for a cup of tea and biscuits (which is what the British call cookies). Nikki joined me after a few minutes, and we both went over our list of purchases. We then decided to go to the container to weigh up what was needed to finish our buying and then take off as soon as we could to return to the inn for a hot bath to warm up after being out in the cold all day.

When we got back, we took off our heavy boots and oilskin jackets, along with our ski hats and gloves. We had a cup of tea while counting money that was left to use the following morning. Then it would be off to Jacque and David's at Hathersage by train the following afternoon. There we could relax and walk the dogs to the pub, which was situated by the river that went through the village. We would have a quiet evening that night; both of us were tired, and we decided that we would sleep in a little later in the morning before packing our cases and checking out. We decided that we would leave the luggage in the van while finishing up the buying for a couple of hours. We requested to eat earlier than normal that evening, and then, after we'd eaten, we went back to our room to get to bed while discussing what we had bought. We both hoped it would mean a successful opening to the season at the Blue Ridge warehouse.

Both Nikki and I woke up in good time to pack, eat breakfast, pay our bill, and say our good-byes; then it was off once more to the showgrounds. We met up with Mick for an update, and we were told the container was almost finished. We gave Mick our suitcases of dirty clothes, insulated boots, and jackets along with the hats and gloves to be packed on the container. We drove the van to the train station to drop off Nikki and the suitcases and then went around the corner to turn in the van. We had a few extra days to visit Jacque and David, winding down our antique-buying trip before returning to Little Gasparilla Island where Julliet was waiting to return to England to continue her studies.

CHAPTER THIRTEEN

 # THE TRIP BACK TO LGI

W E CAUGHT THE noon train to Doncaster for the transfer to Sheffield. Jacque was waiting for us in the Sheffield Train Station terminal; she saw us as we walked down the steps, with a large smile and waving at the same time. We were equally glad to see her again. Our paths normally crossed several times a year in Florida and England; that had been the case for several decades. Jacque informed us that David was at work and asked us if we'd like to stop by his company for a quick visit. "Sure," we said. She drove us to an area of the town that had modern warehouses along with old three-story Victorian red-brick steel mills and where the famous cutlery was made and forged for clients all over the world, famously known as Sheffield stainless steel.

David was waiting for us at the top of the stairs, saying how nice it was to see us again and asking if we had time for a cup of tea or coffee. His two business partners, Terry and Brian, came out of their offices to welcome us to Troika Moldings. Nikki teased them that the area still hadn't changed its salubriousness. Terry advised Nikki not to go for a long walk unless she took one of them as a minder or maybe all three of them, and we all laughed at the thought of walking about in that rough area of Sheffield. After our hot beverage, Jacque thought we should leave and asked David that if he could be home early to entertain their

American friends, it would be extremely appreciated. On the way to Hathersage, Jacque stopped at a large grocery store for us to buy tea, biscuits, and "lockets" to take back to Florida.

We arrived at the Bevans' house and walked into their lounge that had a magnificent view of the Hope Valley down below. The whole wall was glassed in, and it seemed to magnify the lush green farmland and hills along with the gray stone-built cottages. Anyone who has read the Brontë classics will know that they had a theme from the Derbyshire Hills. Emily Brontë, we were told, once stayed at the old vicarage beside the church, on a tall hill overlooking the village; also, the local graveyard was where Little John of Robin Hood fame was buried, with his gravestone being on an extra-long grave. Nikki and I had visited these close friends in that lovely village many times over the years, sometimes for weeks at a time, so Hathersage always seemed a little like home whenever we were there. Christmas Eve mass in the church was really amazing; the midnight celebration of Jesus Christ's birth was something one never would forget. The same can be said about going to the local fate on a warm August Bank Holiday, with the local butcher slow-roasting pork over hot coals, with all the prettily clad girls running through the dandelions and daises and the "little too big" boys playing cricket in the sunshine with their dads.

David arrived home and relaxed with a pint of dark beer. He joined us while we were watching the news from Florida about a northeasterly storm forming out in the Gulf. Jacque suggested that we call Julliet on the island to see if she was okay. Nikki said that would be really good and asked if she could also call Jonathan in Aberdeen, as he had left a message earlier, apologizing for not coming down to help us; he said he was very busy with university. When she spoke to him, she told him that she fully understood, and then asked him if he'd been watching the weather in Florida. He said he wasn't aware of any problems. Nikki then handed the phone over to me, and we talked for a little while, with me telling him to study hard and kidding him that if he did, he would be as smart as his dad one day. I told Jonathan that we would be over in the UK again in June to do more containers, so we hoped that we could see him then. Little did we know he was not attending university at all! He was taking our monthly allowance to live on while we also paid his rent. He was neither studying nor working or even looking to find a job. Later, when we found out all he did was party with his university friends, we were really, really disappointed in his behavior.

Nikki then quickly phoned Julliet and got the update on the weather forecast in Southwest Florida. She soon handed the phone to me so that I could help our dear daughter make plans to evacuate as soon as possible. I told Julliet that her mother and I were very worried about her safety and that Florida storms could not only have violent winds but rising tidal flooding. She told us that George wasn't too worried with what was going on, and I felt a little relieved and agreed that George was a good person to listen to, as he usually knew how to judge these things.

We said our good-byes to Julliet and let her know that we would be at the Clayton's (old friends from Harrow) by Gatwick Airport Sunday night, and we'd then fly out on the early Delta flight Monday morning. I reassured her that I would stay informed about the storm throughout the flight back and would call her when we got through immigration at Atlanta. We realized we would have to run in the airport to connect on the 3:30 p.m. flight so that we could cross the Bay in the daylight; we would let Dick know the time. And we both agreed that we couldn't wait to see Julliet and Napier again.

The weather forecast for Florida looked quite stormy for the next few days. We really did manage to relax at the Bevans' after a week of hectic antique shopping. Jackie made a steak-and-kidney pie with all the fixings, which was scrumptiously delicious! After dinner we adjourned to the lounge with a cup of coffee, tea, or brandy. Jacque said they were looking forward to visiting us on

LGI next month for a few weeks, and we agreed that that would be fantastic as long as we could plan to be off the island by April second or third, according to the weather conditions for crossing the Bay. That would allow us to be back in Georgia for the delivery of our container. After lots of discussions, it was agreed that when we got back to the island, they would be at the beach house within two weeks, hopefully to do a lot of fishing, reading, walking, and crossword puzzles. We all went to bed happy and replete.

After breakfast we got packed and made our way to Gatwick Airport, where we would be staying with the Claytons for our last night in the UK. Our journey entailed leaving from Sheffield Train Station to King's Cross, then catching the Thameslink train, which was just a short walk from the main station in London. We were on time for getting to Gillian and David's house at about 4:00 p.m. David had spent a lot of time in Saudi Arabia for the security company he represented, but fortunately, he was in town that weekend.

On the agenda that night would be just relaxing and bringing in fish and chips. Nikki had the opportunity to spend time with another Harrow girl from her growing-up years. David Clayton had always been a straightforward, no-nonsense man, British from head to toe, and been like a big brother to Nikki when growing up in Harrow. His parents' house was always open to the neighborhood children, and many get-togethers and parties were enjoyed there.

We arrived at their home to an extremely warm welcome with lots of hugs and kisses, and then everyone sat down in the lounge with a cup of tea, going over the past months since our last time together. Katy and Lawrence, two of their kids, were also there, and it was good to see my godson again—he was turning into a good-looking young man! David and I went out for the fish and chips while Jill and Nikki talked about all the people they both knew. After supper, I asked to be excused to go to bed, but Nikki decided she would stay up to socialize with our hosts.

The next morning, David drove us to Gatwick Airport, getting there at eight o'clock for the 9:30 departure to Atlanta. We stopped by the business elite lounge for coffee and sweet rolls, newspapers, plus a few free Delta Airline ink pens to write with on the journey of close to nine hours. I reminded myself to look for Greenland out the right-hand side of the window on the airplane when we passed over it. The service was superb, with lots of food, snacks, and cups of tea, as well as a chocolate sundae for dessert; Nikki would opt for cheese and fruit. After lunch we worked on our container manifest while at the same time discussing the items bought and their salability with the dealers who usually purchased enough to clear our cost. Then the retail customers added to the profit margin, which helped us accrue enough money to hopefully go back the following June on another buying trip.

After all the talking, reading several newspapers, and having a few naps, the trip went by pretty quickly. We arrived at the E-side concourse, and we hurried off the plane to get to immigration before the crowd behind us in order to catch the early Sarasota or Tampa plane, whichever would get us to the dock on time. Immigration with customs went very smoothly, allowing us to make the early flight. We rushed to call Julliet; thank goodness we could use the phone onboard the plane to let her know that we were going to be early into Tampa. It was costly but well worth the ten dollars so that we could get to the island before dark. Julliet would call our friend Dick to say that we were going to be at Eldred's Marina at six that evening.

Dick was there waiting as we drove up, flashing our lights and waving. He was all smiles, with us stepping into his boat, saying to us that not much had happened since we had been gone. He said that he had got there a few minutes early as he enjoyed looking at the different boats, and we thanked him for turning out to give us a ride to the island. It was so good to be on the Bay, smelling the salty air as we headed to dock 88. It seemed that we had been gone longer than the two weeks that it actually was. After getting off his boat and standing on our dock, Nikki asked him if he and Doris would like to visit us the next day for drinks at five.

We were both excited to be walking up the Peacock Lane with a welcoming Gulf breeze; Napier and Julliet were both very glad to see us, with Napier jumping up to be petted and licking our arms. We dropped off our bags and got out of our dress suits to put on our shorts, t-shirts, and tennis shoes to walk on the beach. We also wanted to see if George was on his deck, and although we couldn't see him, the surf was welcoming. We had our drinks with us as we ambled down to the beach, with Julliet asking us how the trip went. We also caught her up on seeing so many of our friends.

Julliet said she was leaving the next day to stay overnight with her friend Missy, then on to Lee and Jimetta's for a night. One of their daughters, Mary or LeeAnne, would take her to Tampa Airport the following morning to fly back to England. We thanked her for taking care of Napier, and she said that the two weeks had been unbelievably good for her. She said it was wonderful to have experienced the solitude and peace that one feels on the island. "It seems like it's just you and the universe, with your thoughts to keep you in tune with yourself." She went on to say how she enjoyed collecting treasures, like shells, sand dollars, and coral, with no one to be accountable to or classes to attend.

We got back to the house to have a small supper, which Julliet had organized. Then it was off to bed for me since we had been traveling for more than sixteen hours, but Nikki decided to stay up to be with her daughter for another few minutes, which turned into a few hours! Napier stayed up with them, hoping for a morsel of food. They were sitting on the porch, so there wasn't any noise filtering into the bedroom to disturb my sleep.

Waking up the next morning at 4:00 a.m., I must have been on British time; I couldn't wait to walk to the dock. In the dark it was so still you could hear fish jumping and dolphins splashing and feeding on the many types of fish available; their blowing sounded like monsters. It was easy again to see the white, sandy lane without a flashlight.

When I got back to the house, Nikki was on the porch, with the smell of coffee permeating through the morning air. With a quick "I love you" and a gentle kiss, she settled into the swing, holding her coffee. After talking over the plans for the day, it was decided that I would do the shopping while I was on the mainland after taking Julliet over. Nikki would stay home to begin preparations for the Bevans' arrival in about ten days.

After breakfast and another walk on the beach, Julliet was packed and ready to go. She walked over to George's for the boat ride that he promised her whenever she was ready to leave the island. It would be a good time to help George with his boxes of heavy goods and groceries in brown paper bags, which were awkward to hold. George usually told the bag boys at Publix (who all seemed as old as he was) to "boat bag everything." (This meant double bags.) And because he had been shopping there so long, most of the time, they did it for him before he even asked.

The bag boys were all retired, always in a humorous mood, and it seemed to be the social get-together place and an escape from doing odd jobs at home. They all hung around to talk after their four-hour shifts were up, when a new crew just as old would take over. Most of them had hearing aids and glasses, and some were even limping while happily doing their job. They had a wonderful attitude, but most of all, they were very helpful. There was something a little strange about an old guy about twenty years your senior, asking, "Do you need help taking your groceries out?" That made shopping at Merchants Crossing a fun thing to do.

Missy picked up Julliet at the grocery store in the middle of Englewood. Julliet was sad to leave her Mom but looking forward to be going back to see her friends at university in England. You could see in George's eyes he was almost as sorry to see her leave as I was, yet I still tried to hide it from her. We went back to the marina in George's car; he always wanted to use his car since he used the more expensive Large Gasparilla Marina, where his Volvo sedan was always parked. The guys there would always help him when he was alone. George always liked to drive his boat fast, making the first turn by the marina sign about a mile from the entrance, leaning to the right, and then he slowed it down when he saw the "No Wake" sign going under the Boca Grande drawbridge. We got back to the dock and tied up George's ropes to the post. I asked him to check the lines to make sure I had made them tight or loose enough not to cause damage during the low winter tides. He always said, "You know what you're doing; I don't need to check your work!"

Nikki was on the beach with the dog when we got back. Seeing us, she hurried over to help George and me carry his stuff up his ramp. We dropped my shopping off at the porch, and she went back to make a cup of tea to have with lunch and check if I had forgotten anything or if there was a nice surprise in the groceries! After putting everything in the fridge and cupboards, we settled on the porch swing to drink our tea and share a Cuban sandwich.

Nikki said there was a letter from Julliet left on her bed, thanking us for a wonderful experience and describing the scary snake episode as well. It read as follows:

> While I was lounging on the front porch glancing over the railing, there was a black snake approximately six foot long. It was staring at me, flicking its tongue, and had no intention of going anywhere else. I dropped some small seashells on its head, trying to encourage it to move away. He was so big; the shells

seemed to be no deterrent. Being scared to my stomach—it was in knots thinking he may come inside the house. I just wanted to call my daddy to help me. After Daddy told me the black snakes eat rodents and poisonous snakes and are welcomed residents in Florida, I felt better; they are evil-looking but harmless to people. After having talked to him over the phone while he was in England, I could not believe what happened next; the snake slid up a tree and swallowed the other snake and then went on his merry way. Other than the snake episode, along with one bad-weather weekend, this place was rare indeed.

It was a great letter and would have been a wonderful entry in her diary.

I took a short nap before we joined George on his deck for drinks at sunset. He had told me in the boat, "From now on, your favorite wine will be on hand!" He also had a case of scotch for Nikki that would last until we left at the end of March or the beginning of April. George was so generous to all who visited him. We both got ready to walk over after feeding Napier. This was the second night home from England, and it was hard to equate the winter there to the winter in South Florida. After sunset, we said good night to George and headed back to cook potatoes and chicken with sides from the deli. We were still jet-lagged and tired, so after a quick supper and a final walk to the dock with the dog, it was time for bed.

I was up early the next morning and put the coffee on while letting the dog out before breakfast. Nikki was slowly waking. We were a little later that day by one hour; I guess 5:00 a.m. was not too bad. Julliet should be calling that morning from England to let us know that she was home safely and how her journey went.

After breakfast our goal was to walk to the southern end of the island, three miles away. There is a small pass to the Gulf from the Bay that separates LGI from Gasparilla Island (or Boca Grande). The little piece of land between is called Shell Island by the locals because of the amount of seashells pushed in by storms and the tides from the Gulf rushing into the Bay. More often than not, we would walk the other way to pick up freshwater in the state park, where there was less chance of finding anyone else collecting shells.

After one particular cold front producing a storm that brought in continuous raging waves for three days, shells were stacked up to over a foot high for miles. There was a bounty of sand dollars, starfish, larger-than-normal sharks' teeth, and large horse conch shells were everywhere. Crab traps would be beached with crabs caught inside. On one particular excursion, we freed a dozen crabs in one cage while working our way down toward the south end, where there were more to free and be allowed to live another day.

After our walk, Napier was ready for a drink of water, and we were ready for a cup of tea on the front porch. Before lunch we walked down to see June, whom we hadn't seen since getting back Monday night. June said her daughter Judy was coming in that weekend and asked if we would like to take the boat to the Ship's Lantern for lunch on Saturday with all the dogs. We thought it was a great idea and suggested meeting on the beach at sunset that evening. We went back for lunch and an afternoon nap for me. Julliet had left a message on the answer phone; she was tired but had made it back without a hitch. Nikki would call her back during my nap. George waved for me to come over while we were sitting out on the porch.

I didn't want to keep George waiting; he needed assistance putting water in the seven batteries in the golf cart. It was awkward, holding the seat up while opening the battery cells. We were then invited to join him on the deck at sunset, and we asked if we could bring June and her daughter Judy along. He was delighted and said that Dick and Doris and George and Miriam Young, who had just gotten to the island, would also be there. It was beginning to sound like a party was forming, and who knows who else would drop by!

After taking care of George's cart, Nikki came by to walk the dog on the beach. She wanted to look for sharks' teeth and sand dollars and other little treasures to put in her biscuit tin to take back to Georgia. Walking in front of Buddy and Lorrie's house, their dog Sophie ran down to play with Napier. Buddy tried to call her back to his place, which was a waste of time, with another dog on the beach to play with. He came down to get her and stopped to talk for a while. We both did so enjoy his conversations, with quips of an optimistic love of life. Lorrie was waving to tell Buddy there was a phone call for him. We took our leave to get home to shower and get ready for the sunset party and also to put together cheese and crackers for our contribution to the gathering.

June came up the steps, drink in hand, with her daughter Judy and, of course, her two dogs. Nikki told her we were all invited to watch the sunset on George's deck. June said she would go home to fix something, and Nikki said we would put a few more crackers on the plate and that would be enough for all of us. Everyone showed up at the same time, and while we were on the deck, Ed and Louise drove up with a plate of Ed's famous smoked ribs, so it turned out there was loads of food. The Sassers' son Robert's dog, Snook, came along with them. All the dogs were well behaved while waiting for the rib bones. We enjoyed meeting June's daughter Judy, and she said she was looking forward to going to the Ship's Lantern on the water the next day by boat.

We all left about the same time, some in carts and some on two feet. Nikki and I walked toward the dock to see what was going on at the Bay. Fish were jumping, a few boats were coming in for the weekend, and Jerry and his wife, Ruth, were just pulling alongside when he shouted for me to catch his line as he threw it, to tie his boat to the forward post. He could then put the engine into reverse to draw the rear next to the dock. After a few pleasantries we all walked back to our respective houses.

There was a message on the answering machine from the Bevans to say that they would be arriving on Friday; they were being driven down to Eldred's Marina by Lee and Jimetta after spending Thursday night with them. They asked if we could arrange the boat taxi for approximately 2:00 p.m. We went to bed excited about having Jacque and David stay with us for a month.

We all used to double date in London in 1967 before we all got married, and we have kept very close through the years. Sleep came early, only to be awakened by Napier hearing a raccoon on the front porch. The early morning was a little cool and very quiet except for waves gently lapping onto the shore. Napier was back to get a little more sleep and hopefully me too.

After a few more hours we both woke up to sit in the cool morning air, sipping coffee and listening to the dog crunching her breakfast. It was going to be a treat to go out to lunch on June's boat. She was very capable and also energetic for someone seventy-plus years. An ex-pilot, she also was very astute in running a boat by herself, and when leaving South Florida in March, she would drive to Maine with only her dogs for company. The Brits would call June "a game ole bird"!

After breakfast, we went to look on the beach for sharks' teeth again (it was becoming an enjoyable hobby). We were simply keeping busy until our outing, which was scheduled for noon. There was time to go back to the house for a cup of tea and a digestive biscuit, which we had brought back from the UK. They go so well together; it was a treat!

Napier and I walked to the dock, meeting Judy halfway down the lane when she told us that they would like to leave in thirty minutes if we were ready, so I turned around to let Nikki know that we were on countdown. We met up with June and Judy at the dock; we were all a few minutes early. Nikki asked June if it was possible to have the dogs at the restaurant, and she simply replied that we would boat to another one if they didn't like our puppies!

CHAPTER FOURTEEN

🐚 SUNSETS, FISHING, AND FRIENDS 🐚

T HAT WAS TO be our first trip down the Intercoastal Waterway since being there; we had crossed it many times to get to the island. Now we were actually going up the waterway toward Englewood. Most of the trip was in a no-wake zone, which meant going slow, which gave us a chance to see many different types of birds sitting in the mangroves, from the great white egrets to different shades of pelicans—brown to pure white. Large blue herons were wading on the edge of the shore, and dolphins were feeding and playing close to our boat. It was absolutely thrilling to us to see from an opposite side, the three islands grouped together by a mega hurricane now on the left of us and the mainland on the right. The three dogs were up front, looking over the bow, scaring Nikki a little. We passed Cape Haze with their modern homes and condos with yachts and fishing boats at their docks; some of them had luxurious sitting areas with outside kitchens.

There was a sign on the edge of the Intercoastal, telling us to turn there for the Ship's Lantern. A very small channel on the right with oyster beds had to be navigated through to get into the restaurant area, which had a small marina. It mainly serviced the beautiful Mediterranean-looking condos, white outside with terra-cotta roof tiles and wrought iron railings, bending around to the right. We pulled in to a designated parking slip beside a charter fishing boat called *Red Man*, which had a party of four men and women unloading the fish they had caught on a half-day fishing excursion that morning: huge grouper, amberjack, along with other smaller fish. I was curious as could be, and Judy asked me what I thought. I immediately said, "Let's book this guy to take us out!" Judy was game, until we found out his price—too rich at that time for us. Maybe next year, if business was good. He gave us his card, just in case.

The four of us sat on the outside of the main wraparound bar area with an open-plan restaurant to view the water, at the same time keeping an eye on our dogs in the boat. The outside was bright and overlooking the water, with the pristine white condos in the distance. It was a beautiful day even though there was a slight chill in the air; however, there was rolled-down, heavy clear plastic to keep out the cool breeze. June and Judy ordered a Bloody Mary, with Nikki having the same, and they were all now soul mates! "And iced tea for me," I said while thinking about possibly driving the boat back, if needed. We all ordered fried shrimp and grouper bites with fries and coleslaw. It was a really neat place and not too expensive—what a find, a true treasure to visit in the future.

June disappeared, and we thought she'd gone to the ladies' room, but when the waitress appeared and Nikki said, "Lloyd, pay the bill," she said it had been settled. We said to June, "We used your boat to get here, so let us pay for the meal. That is the least we can do."

June said, "Maybe next time."

I thought to myself we would have to get up earlier in the morning to outfox June. Wonderful food, tremendous company, and then it was time to make our way back down the Intercoastal and across the Bay to dock 88. The dogs had been accepted as long as they stayed onboard; we rewarded them with a few French fries. It had been a very relaxing afternoon, especially for the three ladies since only one of us didn't have a couple of real drinks. Even so, June and Judy were more than capable to captain the ship.

June asked me if I would I like to take us back. I couldn't wait to drive the boat, and still being a little apprehensive on driving a strange vessel, I was probably a little too cautious. That was the first time for me since my boyhood days, and not often then, to go somewhere by boat, much less take full control. June's boat the *Sandwitch*, with its Yamaha outboard, handled like a Cadillac. Even Nikki was enjoying the ride; for someone who didn't like traveling on any type of water, that was exceptional. But when Judy said, "Lloyd, why don't you park the boat?" the look on Nikki's face said, "Maybe that was not a good idea." Thinking about the possibility of docking without mishap had been on my mind for the whole hour. I was just about to get up to hand her the controls when she said that, unbeknownst to us, they were setting me up for using their boat whenever we needed transport to go across the Gasparilla Sound.

Back at the dock in shipshape order, we tied it up and disembarked. Then we all walked together back down Peacock Lane. When we arrived at June's house, we said, "Thank you again, and hope to see you tomorrow." We got back to our place, and it was time for a late nap; an hour later, Nikki brought me in a cup of tea while I slowly woke up.

Nikki told me that she had called Julliet and Jonathan in the UK to catch up on their activities. Both were doing well, it seemed, and enjoying the weekend with no classes to attend. It was getting close to five and almost time for drinks at sunset, to be followed by a stroll on the beach.

We walked past George's house, and he was sitting on his deck by himself. He shouted, "Your drinks will be ready by the time you climb the ramp!" There was a soft, warm breeze coming off the Gulf now, not at all like that morning. The sun was almost down, throwing light into wispy blue clouds, turning the edges silver with a few shreds of gold—truly spiritual. We all just watched without having to speak throughout the sunset. We said good night to George and that we would see him the next day at the same time. He said that he would be there and not to forget that our drinks were ready and waiting so not to bring anything with us. We both answered, "It's a date."

On the way back to the beach house, Nikki said she would go with me to take Napier to the dock for her last walk before bed. Bob and June Shirley were on their porch, asking if we wanted to join them. Nikki replied, "Just for a minute or two as it has been a long day."

Bob said, "Yes, it has, we saw you leave on the *Sandwitch*. Where did you go and how was the ride?"

I replied, "We all had lunch at the Ship's Lantern, where the food was great, and the trip went very smoothly." He asked us if we would like a drink, but we told him no, thank you, as it was getting late for us, and we haven't gotten used to being on the time zone again, for some silly reason. They were really nice country folk (or what locals call Florida Crackers).

It was back to the house to get ready for bed; we were still full from lunch and the sausage and crackers on George's deck. There was a message from Ed and Phyllis Strickland on the answering machine; they wanted to visit the next day for a couple of days to see what the island was all about. The water taxi had been booked for noon, which meant they should be at our dock by half past twelve or one. Ed worked for Delta as a jet aircraft maintenance technician at Tampa International, where he met his wife, Phyllis, a strikingly beautiful rental-car agent with very wispy blond hair and a friendly, outgoing personality. We were going to be busy little bees for the next five weeks on LGI. It was off to bed for another early start to get the house and beds ready again for guests. We were both asleep almost simultaneously—it must have been the salt air. Anyway, what a luxury it was, to be able to unwind in a comfortable bed.

Napier got us up a little earlier than normal, but we really didn't mind. We think she knew we were very happy about having more company coming in that day, and that made her excited. We must have given off good vibes. After breakfast, we took a walk down to the beach with her, and then we got busy. I was given the jobs of vacuuming, mopping, and then my favorite—sweeping the front and side porch, while Nikki was in charge of everything else. Once we had finished our chores, we had a cup of tea on the porch. Phyllis called from Publix in Englewood to see if they could pick up Sunday lunch, and Nikki again suggested a rotisserie chicken with a couple of sides, as it was the easiest and everyone liked that meal. Then I heard her say that she would see them in an hour and looked forward to spending time with them.

We set off early to wait at the dock, stopping on the way to talk to June and Judy, who were working in the yard, planting a few flowers and shrubs. They wanted to know what we were doing, and we told them about our friends arriving at the dock soon by taxi. They said they would have gone over to pick them up for us. We thanked them, but we couldn't possibly impose on them. It was such a time-consuming chore, especially when we had so many visitors. They said that, next time, they would love to do it. "How nice was that?" we said to each other while walking on toward the dock to meet Ed and Phyllis. We didn't want to tell June about the Bevans and the Andersons arriving, hopefully, on Thursday or the Stricklands returning on Tuesday. We couldn't get over how nice June and Judy were, giving themselves up to help us out in any way they could.

When we arrived at the dock, we noticed that the taxi was halfway over, just making the turn by marker 7 to head due north toward us. Sam, we were sure, was piloting the taxi, and as they got closer, we could see Phyllis waving and yelling, "Where are we, Lloyd Boy?" As they pulled alongside, Sam asked Nikki if she felt like an islander yet—even though her accent said maybe not. Sam had, like everyone else in the South, found Nikki very warm and giving. I must say, as her husband, she was always classy and lovely.

The Stricklands stepped onto the dock, and you could see they were pleased to be there by the look in their eyes. Ed said, "All right, boy, tell me how you found this place?"

As we walked up the Lane, I said, "Well, Ed, a guy called Tommy told me about a little island where he and his wife, Amber, had a summer home—"

We were interrupted by the sound of the surf. Ed and Phyllis commented on how one could walk from the Bay to the beach in such a short time! They were delighted by the sight of the Gulf and the sound of the waves.

Inside the house was the next surprise. Ed said, "Boy, you did well. What a place!"

We took the luggage and shopping inside when Phyllis noticed how basic the beach house was, but she told Nikki that she loved it anyway. We said that we really enjoyed staying there and how fortunate we were to have found the island and have friends who would let us stay in their beach house. While I put things away, the girls prepared the meal for us all to help ourselves and eat outside. The Stricklands loved hearing the soft roar of the waves while having lunch. After lunch we walked about an hour south on the beach, showing them on the way George's place, Buddy and Laurie's house, and the condos farther down the beach. It was amazing to them that there was no one to be seen for miles on such glorious sand.

When we got back, Ed had photos from the last Golden Boot Awards in Hollywood; he has always been part of that charity organization. He wanted to show us the movie stars they were photographed with along with the Delta employee volunteers who made up the security team. I excused myself to take a nap before the five o'clock ritual on George's deck. Nikki was a real trooper to sit through all the photos; I loved Ed like a brother, but photos weren't exactly my way of spending a couple of hours.

We all had to get ready for sunset at George's; Nikki wore a full-length mauve dress with a sea creature decoration on it. Her favorite dress was sun yellow with a beach-chair motif, and Phyllis looked gorgeous in a beautiful blue beach dress. Most people wore some type of fishing or beachwear at sunset or dinner parties on LGI.

The Stricklands, like everyone else, fell in love with old George. He told them all about how he found the place thirty years ago when there were two houses in front of his and now his was seafront. He told them how his wife, Ingrid, who was so dear to him; his blue eyes would sparkle when he spoke her name. He said, "Let's go fishing tomorrow morning, but not too early, say about ten or soon after."

Ed and I said, "Yes, thank you, we would love to go with you." After a few more stories, a few drinks, and the sun finally setting, it was time to walk the dog and head home for bed. We were all exhausted and ready for sleep.

Lying in bed, Nikki mentioned that George's sister Gussie was coming in next week for a short stay to do some fishing and to get away from the cold in Rochester, New York. She was younger than George and a retired schoolteacher, married to George's brother, who had passed away a number of years ago. We were looking forward to meeting her, and it was going to be busy for the next few weeks with all our company. She also said Jimetta called that morning to see if it would be all right for the Delta group to come down again for a weekend while Jacque and David were on the island (the same group that came down to spend a few days with the McGills). They had found a place to rent that would accommodate four couples from Friday to Monday. Melodie Daniels was the only one that wasn't retired, and she had to be back at work on the ticket counter Monday morning, so she and Dick would have to book the water taxi for Sunday night around eight. All these guys knew Jacque and David from all their visits to the UK and in Florida throughout the years. We thought that would be wonderful to have everyone together again.

The next morning, Ed, Napier, and I woke up before the girls; we had to tiptoe to the kitchen. While Ed opened the door to let the dog out, he said they had brought their own coffee percolator (it looked like it was from the sixties) because Phyllis liked to brew it her way. After making the coffee, we walked to the dock to see the sun rise. Napier was chasing something in the trees, most likely an armadillo, which really she should not get close to because they could be vicious with their back toes if they felt threatened. The sunrise was quite beautiful shining over the Bay—a sight I never tired of.

Ed said it might be good to go back to the house since we had left almost an hour ago. The girls should be up and hopefully fixing breakfast by then. They were sitting on the porch when we got there, and Phyllis said, "Where have you boys been?" and Ed replied, "Watching a spectacular sunrise." We all thought that, after breakfast, we would walk on the beach. As we slowly ambled on the white sand, we looked for seashells for the Stricklands to take back to their house in Floral City. Going back to the beach house, we saw George on his deck and stopped to see him to ask what time we should be ready to go fishing. He said to just give him about thirty minutes to find the appropriate rod and reels for trolling in the Boca Grande Pass and he would be ready to go.

Ed and I had to cover ourselves with sunscreen, for the sun would be pretty strong, especially out on the water because of the reflection. We packed cold water, colas, Ed's Budweiser beer, and sandwiches for everyone. George was outside in his golf cart and told us that he was ready to go. After getting the gear onto his boat, we were off, cruising under the bridge, then down the Intercoastal, to the south end of Gasparilla Island to troll close to the old phosphate docks.

We set the lures out, and within minutes, we landed a twenty-five-inch grouper; however, it would be another hour before catching an additional keeper. Then George said that, as we had enough for supper, we should go home, apart from the fact that he was getting tired of driving the boat (you can only go five knots when trolling) and needed a rest. While George navigated the way back, Ed sat in the other chair up front, and I held on to both chairs for stability since George had the throttle as fast as it would go. He was shouting that we would cook the fish at his house just after sunset. "That sounds good to me," Ed replied. We ate our sandwiches on the way back as it was hard to eat and pull in fish at the same time. Back at the dock, we filleted our catch and washed down the fish-cleaning station before heading off to the house.

No one was home, so we assumed the girls must have been on the beach, and before joining them, we had to wash and change into clean bathing trunks so that they wouldn't complain about us smelling like old fishermen. As we stepped onto the beach, we saw them approaching us each with a bucketful of beautiful shells. We all wanted to know how and what each of us had been doing for the last three hours. Ed was the first to inform the girls that we were having a fish fry that evening, saying it had been years since his last one. Phyllis said that she was delighted to have all those shells to decorate their screened-in patio. Ed said, "Okay, baby doll, I think they would look really good there." It was time for some refreshment, so we went back to the beach house for a cup of tea and cakes, with Ed saying, "Maybe a cold Budweiser."

We all relaxed the rest of the afternoon away on the porch, waiting to go over to George's for sunset and the fried-fish dinner. Nikki made her barbecue baked beans to go with it, and Phyllis prepared the cold slaw and a few nibbles to take along. Heading over at five, George was waiting in his usual chair. When he saw us he said, "What took you so long?" with Nikki quickly saying, "We are on time for a change, George! And we heard you guys caught supper this afternoon."

George replied, "All I did was drive the boat, these two guys did all the catching."

Phyllis said, "They haven't told us much about the fishing trip, what are we having?"

"Grouper, of course, what else would there be?" George replied.

I said, "It was a very good expedition, we caught quite a few fish, but there were only two keepers. The wave in the pass wasn't too bad either."

Ed quickly added, "I certainly wouldn't want to be out there if it was any rougher."

After supper and all the tall fish tails, it was time to say good night to George, and the four of us headed back to our house for a nightcap before bed.

We were all up early the next morning; the Stricklands had been with us for two days when it was time for Phyllis to return to work at their lake home and real estate office on Duvall Island in Floral City, Florida. Ed was now a man of leisure who travelled to Los Angeles twice a month, organizing the Golden Boot Awards. He was also passionate about the NASCAR circuit; always attending the annual Indy 500, which he had not missed for decades, as well as all the famous Daytona races.

On Tuesday morning, with the Eldred's water taxi coming at half past nine, Ed and I with Napier walked the beach while the girls were getting up. Ed told me that he thought LGI was a special place where one could really relax just walking the beach and fishing, and there was time to just sit and think and contemplate life in general, but he also believed that the island was not for everyone because of it being so remote. I told him that I used to be that way; making money was more important to me than anything. Even playing golf was a big part of my life while living in Scotland and being a member of the Alyth Golf Club in the 1980s and early '90s. Watching sports on weekends would control my time, whether it was baseball, college football, tennis, or just about any type of game. My life had changed a lot after being on LGI for a few months. My outlook now was about recharging batteries in the winter and then really working hard during the summer and taking weekends off for entertaining friends. "Well, boy," Ed said, "I'm very happy for you, but now we should be getting back to see if the girls are ready. Phyllis should be packed and biting at the bit to get back to her real estate sales."

We were soon all ready to walk to the dock to catch the water taxi. While walking, Ed said they definitely would be back again and asked if we were planning to return next year. We said that we hoped to as long as the business was doing well and we could afford to take the winter off. While waiting on the dock and looking out over the Bay, we could see, far across to the other side, about a mile away, that a boat was coming out of Eldred's channel. We thought it must have been Sam, on his way to us. Gasparilla Bay was calm, and we watched the occasional dolphin, along with several osprey and quite a few pelicans, feeding. Waiting with our friends on the dock with that activity in the water made the departure a lot more memorable for everyone. Sam pulled alongside, saying to Nikki, "Hey, gal, are these friends of yours, or do they claim Lloyd as a friend?"

She said, "Only because I share my friends with him," in her polished British schoolteacher accent.

We all had a chuckle when Sam said, "Whatever you said, it must be true, the way you said it like that." After hugs and kisses, we waved good-bye to our friends as we had many times over the years in America, England, and Scotland. Ed, for a big man, was always emotional, with a few tears and his voice breaking, whether it was a greeting or a farewell. Walking back to the house, we both felt a little deflated at seeing our friends leave. It always seemed fast and furious when the Stricklands visited, with lots of good food and as much fun.

Back to reality, we had to get ready for the Bevans later on that week, and then the Delta crowd would be arriving. Planning meals was uppermost in our minds and the most important task. Everything else would fall into place since we've all known one another for over thirty years and, in Nikki and Jackie's case, over forty years, and we were all very comfortable. We decided we would have to go to the mainland to do a big shop, and we could give Lee a list for any last-minute things when they bring Jacque and David down. That would save us another taxi fare.

We definitely had to go to the park for water. Shopping excursions had to be carefully planned since the cost for the water taxis had to be added into the food expenses. Therefore, they were kept to a minimum as money was fairly tight at that time; we were still trying to build up the business in Georgia. Small amounts of money saved led to a better investment in the short term with long-term advantages. In the past, we had made lots of money and had been involved in many business ventures and gambles that sometimes turned good and sometimes bad. From then on, we were determined not to gamble again with everything we had. We were getting older, and it was harder to recoup, so savings were a necessary tool to have the chance of making it in business and enable us to continue in our endeavors. Well, anyway, we had to do it our way, right or wrong, as it was a process of trial and error, as life surely is.

Getting ready for the Bevans was exciting. I could see us cleaning for the next couple of days; we both enjoyed working together and had many tea breaks. Since resigning from Delta Airlines in 1981 to start our own business in the United Kingdom, we had worked successfully together through good and many not not-so-good times, with lots of fun always planning for the next year. We would talk everything out with plenty of optimism for the future.

Finally, it was time for lunch and a nap while listening to talk radio, which seemed to help me get to sleep quicker. Dale had introduced me to *Rush* on the radio when we started spending more time in Florida in the winters. He was right; his program was always poking fun at both parties with lighthearted comical scenarios.

As I woke up and turned off *Rush*, Nikki asked if we should go onto the porch with a cup of tea to see how we were going to spend the rest of the day before getting ready to join George at five. Maybe we could venture to see what was new in the library. After the tea and biscuits, off we went.

On the way, Don Fowler, the local real estate agent, stopped by in his buggy to talk to us and see if we were enjoying the island. We both nodded in agreement and said that it was definitely a special place; he said he had seen us around for several months. As he drove away, Nikki commented that he seemed to be a nice guy; I agreed that he did have a quiet, relaxing way about him.

At the library, we found new mysteries for Nikki, and I was able to find a small book on rural Florida. We then went back to the beach house, with plenty of reading material for the next week. David and Jacque also loved to read while on holiday, whereas I tended to repair fishing nets or restring reels. After getting ready, Nikki made her favorite nachos with melted cheese and salsa. George was already sitting on his deck, waiting for us to show up to discuss what we had done that day. Again the weather was okay, not too cold or too hot, holding in the mid-sixties. We really didn't mind the cooler evenings; it was much easier to sleep. After sunset we said good-bye to walk the dog before turning in ourselves. We went to sleep, talking and planning our next few days before the Bevans arrived. Resting would be a way to get ready.

Waking up the next morning, we knew they were on the way to America. They would stay the first night in Tampa with Lee and Jimetta, as it would be too late to cross the Bay in daylight. We had plenty to talk about that morning on the porch over coffee with our main breakfast staple of whole wheat toast with jam.

We knew that, throughout the day, we would be mapping where the Bevans were until they called us from Tampa. Then we could schedule the water taxi for the next day after their breakfast at the Cuban restaurant on Florida Avenue, about three blocks from the Andersons' house. The Cuban *café con leche* comes with Cuban bread for dunking and grits to keep the Crackers happy!

We finished our breakfast, and then it was time to take Napier for a walk down the beach by George's house to see if he was stirring, but all was quiet except the waves crashing onto the shore. We could see for miles up and down the beach with not a living soul to be seen; again it really felt like we were stranded on a tropical island. So wonderfully peaceful, to have the whole beach to ourselves except, of course, for sandpipers running up and down, teasing Napier. We walked a little longer that morning, up to the park to get a drink for the dog. On the shore at that end of the beach, you can often find coral since there was a crevice running straight out west, where the water is very deep.

We went back to Peacock Lane for a few last-minute chores before lunch and my daily nap. As we walked again by George's house, he was out on his deck, having breakfast. He was a little hard of hearing, so he yelled to us, "The coffee just brewed!" We joined him, which was very enjoyable after a long stroll. George said he was going over to the mainland that day and asked us if we wanted to go with him to do any shopping. Nikki thanked George and said that she would give me a list of things we needed. I said, "You will?" George chuckled, saying he would pick me up in his cart in thirty minutes. "What about my lunchtime nap?" I said.

They both retorted, "You can take it later today."

"You are outvoted two to one," George informed me.

I responded with "Okay. I'll be ready in half an hour."

We went back to the house, and Nikki started working on the shopping list. She suggested it would be thoughtful of me to go to George's early and help him load up his garbage by walking it down the ramp. I agreed and mentioned that he also had a lot of water jugs to fill up at the Publix's grocery store filter machine, way too many for him to handle. Between us, we would have about ten jugs—that's a lot of hauling. In a way, it gave me an excuse to help him without telling him he needed help because of his age and difficulty in walking. In most other ways, he did act so young, especially his outlook toward life in general.

With list in hand, I went off to George's to load up his cart, and then we were off to the dock. George got into his boat and then lowered the engine to start it, then he told me to untie the ropes, and I climbed in and pushed us away from the right side of the dock, carefully watching the post that jutted out, since the dock was shaped like a T. We arrived at Big Gasparilla Marina; we left the engine in the up position as that was the clue that we would be returning within the day. The engine left down would tell the Gasparilla dock crew they would need to take it out for storage, and when a boat was done the crew then needed an hour to put it back in the water.

We climbed into George's Volvo sedan and headed for Englewood to go to Publix just a short distance away. One needed patience, shopping with George, as he was not fast, but older people do deserve patience, and the chore usually did get done. We were laden down with gallons of distilled drinking water and enough food to last at least a week for both of us, not to mention extra snacks and goodies for entertaining. We got back to Peacock Lane, and Nikki came down the steps to lend a hand with lugging bags and boxes of provisions into the house. I went with George to help him up his ramp, especially with the water. He said thank you very much and that he would look forward to seeing us at five. I also thanked him for taking me over so we could start to welcome our friends arriving the following day. Nikki had everything put away except the water jugs, which were left on the porch in the shade, to be used as needed.

Nikki had a late lunch ready, after which I finally took my nap! That afternoon, we took the dog for a stroll down the beach, where we met Laura collecting shells—baby's ears were one of her favorites, along with shark eyes. Both are quite rare and hard to spot; we still concentrated on sharks' teeth and coral. It's difficult at first, to focus one's eyes on finding more than one type out of a huge pile of shells.

We cut in land, down Marsh Street, toward the library to see what was happening on the Bay. Then we took Grande Avenue to Peacock Lane to go back to the house, passing June's place, where she was out filling the dog's water bowl up with the water hose. Nikki was tentative about letting Napier drink June's water, but once again, June told her that she had a reverse osmosis system in the downstairs tool area and anytime we needed water just to help ourselves. We just couldn't imagine someone having their own water-filtering machine. "June, that is so thoughtful."

Nikki responded, "Lloyd goes to the park, and it is good exercise for him, and he might lose some weight!" She went on to tell June about her friends arriving the next day from England. I excused myself to get back to see if there were any messages from them en route to Tampa Airport. Nikki showed up thirty minutes later, after having had coffee with June. She said what a thoroughly good person June was, and she had insisted that anytime we would like to use her golf cart, we could just take it for touring the island or picking up stuff from the dock.

It was time to get ready again for sunset with George. He welcomed us to his deck while putting out drinks and snacks on the table. Nikki explained to him who was arriving the following day, that it was a childhood friend and her husband, and they would be staying with us for four weeks. We told George that we had often stayed with them in England on many business trips over the years. They had come to Florida almost every year to stay with us, and when we lived in the UK, we would all take our summer vacations together with our children and go all over Europe to different warm Mediterranean countries.

LLOYD ARTHUR WIGGINS AND ROSEMARY EGERTON LETTS

After sunset we walked the dog before having a light supper. Jimetta called while we ate, to say the Bevans had landed and were relaxing by the pool while Lee was barbecuing and that Ed and Phyllis were also there to welcome them back to Florida. Nikki spoke to Jacque, who excitedly asked about the island. Jet lag takes a backstage when a party is being held in your honor. Nikki could tell by Jacque's voice their anticipation of discovering LGI, especially with the many places to fish, either from a boat, the beach, or the dock. Jacque absolutely loved fishing, and Nikki had told her about friends with boats who would take her out to troll for king mackerel, grouper, or ladyfish. That was the most fun—waiting in a boat chair while the line is being set out while going approximate four to five miles an hour. We knew when we woke up the next morning it would only be a short time before they were there, so it was off to bed after another tiring day.

I was up early enough to take Nikki her coffee in bed, which was always greatly appreciated. After the Bevans got there, it would probably be every man and woman for themselves in the bathroom and the kitchen. Breakfast, as it was most days, was on the porch, and then we took a half hour walk on the beach—just biding our time before the phone call to say that they were on their way. The water taxi had been booked for early afternoon. Nikki walked to June's to see if we could use her cart for the luggage, which would be huge and heavy, knowing how Jacque and David travel.

The British always seem to have the largest, most cumbersome luggage of anyone in the world after looking at passengers waiting in line at ticket counters in London or America. It's not hard to spot the Brits! Nikki was back after having coffee with June, and I was off for an early nap to get energy for later! Nikki could not understand how anyone could take a nap when things out of the ordinary were going on. A little later, I was up and ready for a quick bite before going to the dock. I never minded waiting there, because it was so serene and beautiful. Napier and

I walked early, leaving Nikki still in the house, doing last-minute things and getting antsy waiting for her friend of forty years to show up on the island. Even though it had only been a few weeks since we saw them in Hathersage, she was still excited to be seeing Jacque again, especially there on LGI.

Jimetta called from their cell phone to say they were in Englewood at the grocery store, and she asked if we needed anything. Nikki confirmed that we had everything and that we would see them on the dock within the hour. We called Eldred's and asked Ruthy to have Sam ready in about thirty minutes. I looked down the lane and spotted Nikki driving the golf cart. Napier rushed off to hopefully get a ride.

It was much more exciting to wait there at the dock and watch the boats coming in from Eldred's Marina than to wait at the house. We were quite early, so we sat on the edge of the dock on Gasparilla Bay, watching the tide roll away, just like the song said. We had added amusements as we watched ospreys and pelicans dive for fish, and of course, the mullet were jumping all around us. While looking at the wildlife, we would occasionally glance toward the area of the marina to see if there were any boats approaching large enough to be the water taxi.

CHAPTER FIFTEEN

🐚 THE LAST BRITISH LANDING ON LGI 🐚

F INALLY, WE PICKED Jacque and David out coming through the channel using our binoculars. It definitely was them on the water taxi. As they got closer, Nikki started waving, and Napier was wagging her tail, getting more and more excited. The Bevans were waving in return, and soon they were pulling up along the side of the dock.

Sam, in his bare feet and with his Southern drawl, said, "These friends of yours sure do speak funny!" We had known Sam for several months by then and still couldn't get used to the fact that he never wore shoes, no matter where we saw him—whether working or fishing, hot or cold.

As they disembarked and looked around at a tropical setting somewhat resembling a jungle, the expressions on both of their faces said that the place looked something from a story one would read about in *National Geographic*. And there was a questioning look on David's face as he asked if there was electricity and water provided. We told him, as he was standing on the dock with his big smile, that yes, we had electricity most of the time and not to worry about water as we could get it with a little walking and teamwork as we had to haul it back to the beach house from about a mile away. He said that he hoped we were joking in his heavy English accent, and then Sam chimed in by saying that no one had good drinking water on the island. David called out to Jacque and asked her "if this could be like one of those dreaded places we had booked in the past without knowing what we would find or were getting into."

Sam replied, "Don't worry, I will come get you in a month or two." He was chuckling as he drifted away from the dock.

After loading the buggy with several huge pieces of luggage and all the shopping, we were off, looking more like an expedition to a mosquito-infested hellhole than a beach house. From David's expression, it seemed that that was what he was probably thinking. There was no room for David and I to ride, and he wondered how far we would have to walk. Nikki, Napier, and Jacque were on the buggy, driving up the lane fully loaded. David said to me that it was definitely different from the condos at the beach around the Indian Rocks area. I agreed with him that it did take time to get used to the remoteness, and I suggested that he try it for a couple weeks, and then, if they would like to, we could all go to Indian Shores for the remaining two weeks.

Walking though the canopy of sea grape trees and Brazilian pepper trees, he asked, "What's that faint roar I can hear? Is it the sea?"

I pretended not to hear him, as I wanted David to see the view for himself instead of imagining beforehand. When we all arrived at the house with the surf lapping onto the shore and they could see the dark-blue water of the Gulf, the Bevans both said what a wonderful view it was; they loved it so far!

Jacque said to David, "Now can you put your thoughts to this positive scenario—whiling your days away, reading in the hammock, while I fish and walk the beach with Nikki?"

"Yes, absolutely," he said with a big smile on his face.

The Andersons called to say they were on their way back to Tampa and wanted to hear what Jacque's reaction to the island was. Nikki told them that they loved it so far but thought that perhaps the inside of the house would take time to get used to.

Jimetta and the other Delta friends were planning to visit us in a week or two.

After the cases were emptied, we all settled down with a cup of tea on the front porch. After finishing our refreshments, David couldn't wait any longer to walk on the beach with Napier. Nikki and Jacque took the buggy back to June's so that Jacque could meet her. They immediately liked one another, and June was invited to join us for drinks at sunset to show our appreciation for her generosity. After an hour, everyone was back to get ready for the Bevan's first sunset.

George called us on the phone to see if we and our friends were going to join him at five. Nikki said, "We would love to, George, thank you!" She told Jacque and David that the sunset from his wraparound deck was the best view in the area, and it allowed one to move on one's chair, if necessary, to get away from the glaring sun.

David loved the white sand creeping from the beach and going under the stilted houses on the lane heading away from the shore. We told them that some storms brought in so much sand, it had to be shoveled from underneath of the first four houses almost like snow. Bleached white sand was so beautiful, it made things look lovely and bright instead of having the gloom of winter, as it was in some places; we all heartily agreed.

After showering, we put on our beachwear while one of the Bevans was in the kitchen, fixing cocktails. When Nikki heard that, she called out from the bedroom to tell them George would be upset if we took our own drinks with us, because he loved to show off his bartending skills that he had learned as a young man. We were sure he would tell them all about it.

We all were going out the door just as June showed up with her drink. She was the exception; she always brought her own. Nikki told her that we were all invited to George's deck, and June agreed the view was much better over there. You could see the Gulf from Tommy's porch, but the sun was too far to the right to see it go down properly. Jacque noticed that June was taking her drink with her, and I replied that she liked her own concoction, and George knew better than to give June any back talk! With a smile on her face, she understood that no one messed with June, a Texas girl, especially one as lovely as her.

We all ambled over as George was coming out through his screen door with his big grin, welcoming us onto his deck. David and Jacque said how marvelous everything was and that it was so good to be there in Florida on a warm beach, especially when two days ago they were in the middle of the great British winter. There were plenty of hors d'oeuvres, with Nikki and Jacque helping George put them on the table along with our contribution.

The setting sun was once again absolutely beautifully. After it went down and the sky lit up with a multitude of orange and turquoise hues, Nikki asked June and George to join us for a barbecue that evening, but they both said their dinner was already prepared but thanked her anyway. June walked with us down the ramp to her cart, and she asked if we would like to go to the Fisheries Restaurant by boat one day that week. Answering in unison, we all said "We sure would, thank you so much" in our many different dialects, from Southern redneck to posh English.

To celebrate with the Bevans, we had steaks cooked on the kettle grill, with champagne for Jacque; Andre's being her favorite tipple. I am sure she didn't know how reasonably priced that wine was. We were all standing around the coals, reminiscing over the years about how many different countries we had barbecued in, and we came up with seven, spanning over many different trips throughout the last quarter of a century. That time and place would most likely end up to be one of the best if we didn't get on one another's nerves, which would be amazing after spending a month together on a small island. All the steaks were great, as was the four of us being together again.

After supper, we all walked the dog to the dock to show our guests the Bay at night. We walked down the lane with flashlights, and it seemed somewhat primitive, with the white sand reflecting from our torches giving it a serene feeling. We were standing on the dock in the darkness, with no lights except for the ones across the Bay from the houses and their docks. There was plenty of noise in the dark waters, with whirling baitfish and mullet jumping all over. It was very nice to be able to have the Bay only a few yards down from our home as well as being so close to the Gulf and the beach.

We were beginning to feel tired, so we went back to the house, and after saying good night to everyone, David, Napier, and I went to bed while Nikki and Jacque stayed up a little longer, talking on the porch. Going to sleep was never a problem, the only sounds being the occasional hooting of owls and the waves lapping onto the shore.

As always, I woke up early, let the dog out, and put the coffeepot on. Then we went down to the beach for a short walk. There were no lights as none were allowed to shine near the shore because of nesting turtles; it really didn't matter as the sand was so white. We walked back to the porch where David was having a cup of tea. I asked him, "Did you sleep well?"

"Like someone drugged me!" he said.

I got my coffee and joined him on the porch. It was still dark, so I suggested we walk down to the dock to see the sunrise. I mentioned that it could be as glorious as the sunset, as it seemed to come up under the drawbridge on Boca Grande Causeway and sprayed lights up to the sky and onto the water.

We walked down a half hour before sunrise. Nikki and Jacque were still sleeping, but Napier was always ready to walk anywhere any time of day. We could hear the fish jumping and an occasional blow from dolphins feeding on the mullet in the dark. David agreed that they sounded like monsters crashing on top of the water. The sun began rising, and it was well worth waiting for; *glorious* was the word David used. He said it was hard to believe that he was at a place where you could see the sunrise over water and the sunset dipping into water in the same day.

We walked back to see the girls sitting on the porch with the cups of tea and coffee, and they asked us where we'd been. David told Jacque that the sunrise was as spectacular as last night's sunset. Nikki asked us if we wanted our breakfast out there or on the table inside. She said the bread was out for toast and that fruit and yogurt was in the fridge, so whenever we wanted to just help ourselves, it was all there.

We went inside to eat, and Nikki fed Napier. After breakfast, we all went to the beach, looking for shells along with sharks' teeth and sand dollars. Looking, walking, and talking in shorts and swimsuits in the middle of winter felt fabulous to us all. We agreed that we were so lucky to be in Florida, taking full advantage of the wonderful weather and the warm waters of the Gulf of Mexico.

Arriving back at the house, Nikki passed out crossword puzzles to everyone from the *London Telegraph* newspaper that our friends had brought over. That was going to be a daily routine for the next four weeks, with the afternoons for reading, walking, and fishing. David's favorite reading area would be a hammock tied to a tree, with the other end tied to the front porch. My job was to make the tea while I attended to business plans with our customers in Tampa, Austin, and Augusta. After a few hours of quiet time, we broke for lunch, and then there was a nap for some of us. I later got up and walked onto the porch where David was sleeping in the hammock and balancing a book on his stomach. We were all very quiet until he said, "Hello, hello, was I snoring?" Jacque asked if anyone wanted tea, and we all agreed yes, we did. So it was teatime in Florida with tea cakes to make it officially British.

After that, we walked to the dock to find June and Bob Shirley walking up their boardwalk to the house. We stopped to introduce them to David and Jacque, and Bob said, "You *sort of* sound like Nikki."

David said, "Well, what about Lloyd's accent?"

Bob replied, "Lloyd here is totally a Florida Country Cracker!"

Then the Shirleys said they were going to Cabbage Key on Sunday and asked if we would like to go with them. The Bevans said that they would like that, having no idea where it was or in which direction. Jacque said, "Any time we can go by boat, we would love to go with you," and Bob told them that he would be leaving about noon. Nikki mentioned that she and I had things to do the next day, so we asked for a rain check. In return, we asked him if they would like to join us for sunset on the beach, and everyone nodded in agreement.

As we stood on the dock, a few boats were coming in for the weekend. What a beautiful sight it was. Soon after that, Jacque said, "Don't you think we need to go back to get ready? We have to feed the dog as well as prepare our evening meal."

So we all marched back after getting our orders from our Madame District Counselor. After showering and putting on our beach attire, we made drinks in the kitchen, which was always a feel-good time; even though the shower was brown and with the noxious smell of sulfur, it could not detract from our great feeling. Nikki walked over to see if George wanted to join us at the Shirleys' house for sunset, but he suggested we all meet on his deck where we could all sit instead of standing on the beach. Nikki didn't have to be asked twice, and she came back to prepare cheese and crackers. Jacque joined her by getting paper napkins with paper plates for the convenience of not washing up. Bob and June showed up as we were just walking out the door, and June Hicks walked down at the same time. We were now seven strong as we converged on George's deck.

It looked like the sunset was going to be a little cloudy, but you never know; sometimes it can suddenly find an opening in the cloud and be magnificent. We were fortunate, anyway, to be there in that beautiful place with our friends from two worlds. As luck would have it, there was a hole in the clouds, and we were able to see a partial sunset into the Gulf.

After picking up our various goods, we all left to go home; June Hicks walked with us while her dogs Bonnie and Jasper played with Napier. The three of them chased each other and rolled in the deep, soft sand. After supper, we took Jacque and David on a final walk to get ourselves and Napier ready for sleep. It had been another memorable day and with more than enough to do the next day, especially for our friends. Nikki was explaining to them all about the route to Cabbage Key and the restaurant there on the desolate barrier island. I excused myself to turn in and left them all talking on the dark porch. When Nikki came to bed, I was dead to the world, so waking me was not an option.

We all gathered in the kitchen the next morning where coffee and tea were being made with toast, jam, and Marmite (a beef yeast extract from England, which was an acquired taste).Once, one of Jonathan's friends from the Chamberlain High School Golf Team put some on a piece of toast and took a large bite, then he dislodged it quickly with the sound of "Ugh!" and screamed that it tasted like something you scraped off the road.

We were all getting along famously, and the feeling was paramount. The four of us had history, to say the least, from London to Tampa, with all our mutual friends and acquaintances crossing borders and countries, from childhood mates to workmates, or friends of workmates, and to those who had married into a different culture. It had all added much interest to our social gatherings.

At that moment, we were all enjoying that particular time in our lives on that special island, which was a real treasure, even if it was quietly thought about without putting it into words for the fear of appearing wet or soppy. All of us left for a stroll after breakfast as Nikki wanted to show Jacque and David the way to the island's library behind Hoots house on the Bay. We then went back to the park the opposite way; she was really enjoying showing them all there was to do and see on LGI. Part of that came from their growing-up days, when Jacque wanted to be in charge attitudinally, but it was in good fun. They always had a friendly rivalry, and Nikki had loved Jacque throughout the years, in both good times and bad. Their childhood days were full of competition and opposing actions while their mature years were filled with kindness and thoughtfulness of friends and family.

Jacque and David went off with the Shirleys on their boat down the Intercoastal Waterway through Boca Grande Pass, where the water could get very bumpy when the tides changed. The Peace River and Myakka rivers emptied into the Gulf of Mexico, adding volatility to the water. The last time we went through there, Nikki was a little concerned with the choppy water, especially when she found out later that world-record sharks could be caught in the pass.

While they were gone, Nikki made calls to Britain, first to the kids and then to her cousins, whom she had called every month for years, along with her favorite aunt Philly as well as numerous friends. Thank goodness calling was cheap due to a lot of competition between long-distance plans to Europe!

After lunch, Nikki brought me up to date with what was happening overseas while we were having a cup of tea and relaxing on the porch. We walked to the dock to see if the group was back from their boat ride, but there were no signs of them, so we went back up the lane to walk on the beach with Napier and look for more sharks' teeth and shells.

After a couple of hours, we walked down to the dock to see if our friends were back, but as there was no sign of them, we returned to the house to get ready for our five o'clock gathering. While we were getting ready, Jacque and David walked in, full of tales of their day's adventures. We let them get ready for the evening, and then Nikki and I took our drinks outside on the porch. My time with her was always so special, just to know she would guide me with love through our social life and business endeavors as she had done over the past three decades; I was thankful every day and looked forward to the next twenty-nine years with her.

David and Jacque joined us with the story of the marvelous experience that they had had. They also told us that, after lunch, they had gone trolling for mackerel, and on the way back to LGI, they had caught quite a few with a silver spoon lure that Bob had shown them how to use. A couple dolphins had swum alongside the boat while they were returning home, hoping for an easy fish to be given to them. They were amazed that the dolphins came close enough for them to be able to reach over the side and touch them as they kept up with the speed of the boat. They had loved spending time with the Shirleys who showed them different islands like Useppa, where some of the yachts were tied up to long piers and some of the estates even had a float plane on an independent airplane dock. On Cabbage Key, they were shown the large mound of shells where the Indians would discard them through the centuries before the influx of Europeans in Florida.

We were all invited to the Shirleys' the following evening for drinks at five. It should be fairly quiet after the weekend, with the Florida Crackers usually leaving on Sunday with only snowbirds and other retired people left on the island. After supper, we all retired to our bedrooms, wondering what would be ahead for the next day.

It was morning already when Napier heard someone in the kitchen; she was ready to get out the door to investigate in case breakfast was being offered. Nikki asked me to make the coffee. Getting up there was easy as I wore swim trunks during the day and to bed at night, so all I had to do was put on a T-shirt and I was ready for the day.

Jacque was making a pot of tea for her and David; she put the coffee on at the same time for us, knowing someone would soon

LLOYD ARTHUR WIGGINS AND ROSEMARY EGERTON LETTS

be letting the dog out. When she saw me entering the kitchen, she said good morning to Napier first and then to me! I took Nikki her coffee and told her what was going on. I said that Napier was having breakfast on the porch and that David and Jackie were having tea in bed, so I would take the opportunity of getting together information from our clients about how their businesses were doing and then discuss it with her.

Everyone was getting up and getting their own breakfast, with Napier hanging around the kitchen hoping something would hit the floor. We whiled away the day, everyone doing their own thing and looking after themselves; that made having company very easy. We would all get together for our journey down to Bob and June's at five o'clock. They told us not to bring anything to eat that night, for they wanted to give us an island specialty. We could not imagine what that could be as the only plentiful thing on the island apart from fish seemed to be coconuts and sea grapes.

After a lovely, lazy day, we were ready for the evening gathering, and we walked down Peacock Lane toward the dock on the Bay. When we got there, the Sassers were there sitting by the barbecue, and Bob was shucking oysters with June and placing them in the half shell on the grill over the coals. They were very good, leaving a zesty sea flavor in the back of your throat. We all then knew what Florida locals on the island called hors d'oeuvres. David could not eat the oysters after getting very sick once from eating them somewhere in Europe, but he still enjoyed the social scene.

We all had a thoroughly good time and looked forward to doing it again. After saying good-bye to everyone, we were on our way back to fix supper. Once that was over and cleared away, with our tummies full, we were all ready for an early night. Even the dog was asleep early!

The following day was a precursor to the week to follow; we were enjoying temperatures in the low seventies and idling away our time on usual island activities and seeing George, June

Hicks, and the Sassers almost every day, mainly at sunset. The Shirleys had taken off to their home in the middle of the state in the Bartow area, and we looked forward to their return. That weekend, we partied on George's deck with an ever-growing number of island friends. Mackerel was now thick in the Gulf, and George and Dick wanted to take us trolling the following Monday if the weather held.

Monday came, and we waited for the phone call to go fishing that morning, so we stayed close to the house. George finally called to say that they were heading off in fifteen minutes and we were to meet up on the dock. Nikki and Napier came down to watch us go; they would stay home and hold down the fort. After pushing off, we headed toward the Boca Grande Bridge and turned right along the Boca Causeway, through the channel that led to the little pass that separated Boca Grande (Gasparilla Island) from LGI.

Out in the Gulf, we had to go about a mile or so off the shore because of the shallow water on both sides of the pass before turning to start trolling. George and Dick asked us to look for birds feeding on baitfish that were being pushed by larger fish such as Spanish mackerel or silver king mackerel. Dolphins were also feeding on larger fish; it was a real-life food chain. We turned north, back toward our area on the island, when George slowed down for us to put the lines into the water. It wasn't long before we were pulling in good-sized mackerel; dolphins were vying for the same fish. After three-quarters of an hour, we had enough for a feast.

As we looked toward the land, we could see Nikki and Napier looking for shells. We yelled at her, waving as she looked to see, and after a few minutes, she realized who it was and started waving back. As we turned around to go back to the dock, George said he would troll back to catch more fish to give to the Sassers and the Youngs, so we did catch a few extra really good-sized mackerel.

When we finally got back to the dock, Jackie started to fillet the fish, along with the guys. A Harrow girl cleaning and gutting fish was a sight to see—she got messy with fishy things, just like the guys. She did impress George, who called her the Judge because of her volunteering as a magistrate in Derbyshire and Sheffield. There was enough fish to ask the whole lane down to George's that evening since, as always, he wanted to do the frying. Nikki and Jacque volunteered to provide the sides. We stopped to tell June Hicks about the Peacock Lane fish fry, and she was thrilled to be invited along with the Sassers who had watched the activity on the docks and came over to say, "What time is supper?"

We all said in unison, "At sunset."

Louise said she would bring the grits with tomato gravy, which was her specialty, with fried fish as the main course. After cleaning all the fish, we had to have a shower, then a nap for me before getting ready for the feast.

Napier had been fed, and the girls had made their side dishes ready to go over; however, we decided that we would wait to see some of the others show up first. When the Sassers drove by, we all marched over en masse. June drove up with her two dogs as we got there, and she had a cake that she had hurriedly baked for the occasion. George came out of the screen door with his apron on to ask the Judge (Jacque) if she and Nikki could help him serve while myself, Louise, and June set the table on the deck.

The guys told Ed how the fish was caught, and he wanted to know why he hadn't been asked to go along. We told him that the boat was full, and we couldn't take anyone else with us, but I said if I had seen him around, I would have given up my place willingly so that he could go. He said, "Oh brother, here we go with the lies!"

Everyone thought that was really funny, as the only fishing that Ed loved was with Louise. They were the perfect fishing duo, always supplying everyone else with smoked mullet and smoked mackerel.

We were all appreciating that special time David was really enjoying the social gathering and the island, where he said everything felt so casual and laid back. It seemed all we did for a party was to relax in large Cape Cod-style resin chairs on the seafront and have our favorite tipple with nibbles or potato chips with various dips. That night was a little special; the plates of fish were arriving with all the fixings, and everyone tucked in. The fresh fried mackerel was delicious, as were all the side dishes. There was fish left over, so we all took some home for sandwiches for lunch the next day. We were all replete and strolled back to our respective houses; some of us broke off to walk the dogs before turning in.

The evening was turning cooler than normal, and that told us that there might be a cold front coming in from the north, but we wouldn't know since the TV didn't work, and there was a definite lack of newspapers. None of us missed watching the television; there was so much to do and see when you were on the island, whether it was on the beach or the dock or the porch. The bird life was so variable, with rare sightings of the magnificent frigate; the white pelicans that came for the winter, ospreys, shorebirds, and the brown pelicans were all common daily sightings. Bald and sea eagles had been spotted occasionally, but not daily or as frequently as the other species. Manatees and sea cows had been seen in the Bay, especially when the water temperature was over seventy degrees and when the sea life was robust with many baitfish and mackerel moving north.

The rest of the week was spent being busy doing nothing, and we had to ask one another from time to time what day it was. I got a phone call from my mom; she told me that she was having a family get-together after church for Sunday dinner, and we were all invited.

When Sunday arrived, all of us, including the dog, boarded the water taxi and got to Eldred's Marina by 10:00 a.m. for the two-hour drive to Riverview. Lunch was at 1:00 p.m.; there was lots of time for enjoying talking with my four brothers and two sisters and their families. We have always had a special relationship with my sister Prissy and her husband Jerry who helped us more than anyone when Nikki and I first arrived in the USA from England in early 1968.

The Sunday lunch was very Southern cooking, with fried chicken, mashed potatoes, and giblet gravy. Nikki didn't like green beans or okra swimming in broth; however, Southerners loved them all! After dessert of apple pie, we all stayed at the extended table, talking. I pointed out that we had all heroes there: Brother Mike in Desert Storm in Iraq and brothers Fred, Floyd, and myself in the army during the Vietnam conflict.

Fred said, "Wait a minute, Lloyd. We were in Vietnam. You were in Germany for thirty-three months."

I replied, "Yeah, Fred, I would've been with you and Floyd over there if my job wasn't so critical to keeping the peace in Europe."

He said, "Driving a truck?"

"Oh well, Fred, I thought about going to Southeast Asia, and the thought of it was just as good as the deed!" Everyone got a laugh out of that.

Nikki said, on that note, we had to go to get back to the island before dark. Avery's wife, Kathy, wanted to know where LGI was, as she said they loved going to the Nokomis, which she believed was not far away. I said that it was true and we would love to see them—if not that year, since time was short, maybe the following one. David and Jacque chimed in, saying they would definitely be back as it was such a fantastic place. After hugs and kisses, we all departed, saying in the car that we all had a warm feeling of closeness at the Wiggins home; we all certainly ate too much!

Back at Eldred's Marina, it was good to see Sam on the dock waiting for us. Ruthy took our fare, and I walked through the store to go out the other side, and off we went across the Bay. We thought that we just might catch the sunset! Napier, like always, was first into and off the taxi. She loved boats almost as much as riding in golf carts.

We were standing on the beach as the sun was a few minutes from setting. "Lovely," David said. There was a message from Jimetta on the answering machine. They were coming to the island for a few days with the Boyettes, Stricklands, and the Daniels that Friday. Time was getting shorter; the snowbirds were packing up to head north, and June would be leaving in a few days with her two dogs, driving all the way to Chamberlain, Maine, after stopping by Judy's house in Tampa for a few days. George Geier and George Young went to the mainland to shop at the hardware store for items like foggers to set off in their houses to keep roaches or other types of bugs out when they left. That would be their last trip to the mainland for that winter. It gave us all a chance to bring drinking water back with other basic necessities to keep us going for the final couple of weeks.

Nikki and I would be leaving for our home in the mountains a few days before George. We could not believe how fast the winter had gone, but we were excited to meet our new antique shipment from the shows in England and also to be back at Lake Nottely with our friends there. It was going to be interesting to see how much we would sell that summer!

Our hopes were to be able to go to the United Kingdom another three times on buying trips if our sales were good and our clients had a need for more antiques. Then I might have to go as early as the following month to buy and load the containers. Jimmie Johnson in Scotland was already storing furniture for me, so the task would be easier if there was at least half of what was needed already in the warehouse. Again I had an early night, while Jackie and David, with Nikki, stayed up a little later than Napier and me.

We were up first the next morning, and I put the coffee on before walking with the dog on the beach before sunrise. I stopped, once back at the house, for a cup of coffee to take down to the dock to see the sunrise. No one was stirring as we crept out the door onto the porch then down the lane. Napier always stayed close to me, especially in the morning gloom or during darkness.

David arrived just before the sun came up, and we both sat on the edge of the dock with our feet almost in the water. He said he was glad they had not spent the last two weeks at Indian Rocks as LGI had grown on him. I agreed and said that John Wade's view was that one could get really "sorry or lazy" about working after a few weeks here! I thought to myself, he may have had something there; however, it was a nice sort of sorry. The sunrise was glorious, and once it rose over the bridge, we went back to the house to see if the girls were up.

Napier hadn't had breakfast yet, so she was going faster than us up the lane. The girls were on the porch as we walked up the steps, and they told us that fresh coffee and tea were in their respective pots and that the bread was out, ready for toasting, with jam and Marmite on the side with the margarine or butter.

The conversation on the porch was all about our island agenda that week, and we all agreed to just enjoy every second of our time remaining. We were even thinking about going in for a swim since the water was a little warmer. I must admit, though, it still felt cold to me when it was in the midseventies; when the outside air was warmer, it made the Gulf seem colder.

Jacque said that when Lee and Jimetta came down early next week, they would go with them to shop a few days before leaving for England. Nikki couldn't believe how fast the time had gone by. After breakfast, we all walked down to the beach, still talking about their holiday and all the new friends they had made as well as the wonderful fishing experiences, with the fish being so plentiful.

We all had a giggle when June Hicks said one evening, "You know what the best bait is, apart from shrimp or greenback fish? Greenback dollars! Publix grocery store will let you have as much as you want, as long as you have enough 'bait'!"

We reflected on what had been said and done in the last twenty-something days. It was hard to believe that we were never bored although we really did nothing except read or do crossword puzzles, collect shells, and socialize, and we never wanted to be anywhere else. We still had four days to ourselves before the influx of ex-Delta workmates came for a long weekend.

Back to the house, I attempted to mend the cast net that was found underneath the house, partially covered by sand; it was a miracle that it wasn't rotten. Thanks to George, I learned how to throw it and do it without clenching my teeth as many Floridian Crackers do.

After a light lunch and a little rest, we were all on the beach braving the water for a swim. Nikki wanted to wade in slowly up to her knees, as did Jackie, but David and I decided to get it over with by diving straight into the waves. The sand mixed in the waves was a little uncomfortable but was still good, and we loved the heavy taste of salty, sea weedy water. We got used to the temperature after a few minutes; by now, the air was feeling warmer too. Napier joined us in the water, with her paws flailing wildly, so we had to stay away from her to avoid injury; she ended up covered in wet sand.

When we got back to the house, we hosed off the dog, and all of us wanted to take a shower and get ready to see George at sunset. That was to be our island agenda for the remainder of the week. The following four days were over before we knew it, and we were waking up Friday morning, getting ready for the Delta group, which would be arriving just after noon and moving into rented accommodations a few doors down from us toward the Bay. Jimetta was bringing Cuban sandwiches for lunch and chicken cacciatore for supper; all we had to do was to make the salad. I suggested that we borrow someone's golf cart to transport the groceries, luggage, and water to their rental house, so Nikki said that she would ask June, even though she was busy getting ready to leave the following day. In return, I would volunteer to help move the luggage boxes from aboard the *Sandwich* into her vehicle at the big marina. Everyone on the island tended to help each other, probably because, in a community like that, being so isolated, it brought out the best in all of us. There was time for a quick early nap before the busy afternoon. It would be hectic yet lots of fun, reminiscing over the past three decades covering America, England, Scotland, and South Africa, along with our many visits to Las Vegas on Delta employee passes.

It was suddenly time to go to the dock to meet the group. Nikki had June's golf cart parked in front. All three girls, including Napier, were on the golf cart, with David and me following behind hurriedly down the lane. We were a little early on the dock; that was a good thing as we saw the water taxi approaching about two hundred yards away, going slowly so as to not make waves. Since it was so close to the shore, it had to abide by the no-wake policy, which is an unwritten courtesy to others on the shore.

They were all waving as they got closer, and Sam pulled alongside the front of the dock. Napier tried to jump on, and Sam yelled at the dog to say they were letting cargo off, not taking any back! So Nikki controlled the dog with a laugh. As always, Sam was intrigued by her accent and her quick wit.

With everyone on the dock, we gave hugs and kisses and welcomed them back to the island. And Ed Strickland said to me, "Boy, what have you been up to? Done any fishing?"

David spoke up quickly and said, "When he's not fishing, he is mending the net for the next throw, sometimes as early as four thirty in the morning. It seems a man has to do what a man has to do to catch fish!"

We all had a chuckle. We loaded up the buggy, leaving room for Nikki, the driver, and her trusty sidekick Napier.

On the way to our house, we dropped the bags off at Ernie Cooper's house next to Jerry's and June's. It was very nice of Ernie to let them use his place so that we could all be on the same lane. Also, Jerry told us that if we needed to use his place anytime, we knew where the keys were—how generous the island folk were!

After off-loading, they all joined us on our front porch for a cup of tea or coffee and the Cuban sandwiches, which were enormous! There was lots of talking, naturally, since we were all close friends. Trying to listen to the different topics was enjoyable with the ability to hone in on a conversation that may be interesting to any part of the group. However, when Nikki talked, all the other conversations seemed to cease, maybe to hear what was on the agenda for the weekend. First thing she said was, "Lloyd, please take June's cart back and ask her to join us this evening for sunset on the beach."

I thanked June for the use of her cart, and then she said in her Texas drawl, "I'll see you on the beach at five." I told her that we were going to miss her after the next day and thanked her again for her generosity. I got back to the beach house just in time to join the others for a walk.

Dale and Mary had their new puppy with them. I teased Dale that his dog wasn't keeping up, which made Dale pick him up, and I said to Dale, "You look like a sissy with a pup in your arms."

He replied, "In a few years, he will be taught to give you a bite if you are mean to me."

"Why, Dale, I've known you for almost three decades. I can't believe you like the dog more than me."

He replied, "I liked him more than you within the first three minutes."

Everybody was telling Dale not to let me give him a hard time. And so it went on; the weekend was like that, a lot of fun with teasing each other and plenty of time spent on George's deck at sunset with him being the perfect host, as always.

The weekend just flew by! Dick and Melodie left the island first as Melodie had to get back to work on the Delta ticket counter, and then, soon, it was time to say good-bye to everyone else, including Jimetta, Jacque, and David, who were going to stay with her and Lee before flying out Wednesday for Derbyshire. Nikki told them that we would see them in June while we were on another buying trip. After hugs, kisses, and tears, we said our farewells and walked solemnly back to our winter beach house, not saying much, just reflecting on the last several days with all our friends.

Back on the porch, we had a cup of tea, contemplating our island departure in a few days' time. That would give me enough time to go with George the next day to take things we didn't need packed in the car so that we would not be overburdened on the last morning. That way, most of our suitcases were packed, and all we had to worry about was ourselves and the dog. While we were at George's that evening at sunset, we told him that we had some shopping to do the following day in Englewood, so I wondered if I could go with him. He said that if I could be ready by nine, there would be no problem. I thanked him for that, and after the sun had set, we went back to the house to pack.

There was a message on the answering machine from Jacque thanking us for the marvelous holiday and saying that they were now in Tampa with the Andersons, enjoying a barbecue and lounging by the pool. That night, on the island, we had a few leftovers for supper, then we went back to packing so that the last few days on the island could be relaxing.

The next morning, I walked several times to the dock with our gear so that George wouldn't have to wait for me. We took off on his boat and went first to the big marina to load up his car, which was parked there, and then we dropped our luggage off at Eldred's Marina, and I eventually loaded it in the Blazer. After doing the shopping, we got back to the island where Nikki and Napier were waiting. During our remaining time on LGI, we took many walks on the beach and down to the dock; those pictures in our mind were going to have to last until next winter. And we spent some time with George; it was now just the three of us in the evening.

Finally, we were to leave the following morning. George got up early to take us to Eldred's, and we left dock 88 at 8:00 a.m. Loading up the boat was a breeze because of our earlier preparation. Looking back for a last look of the place we had grown to love was a mournful feeling; the mood in the boat was very quiet. As we pulled alongside Eldred's dock on the right, Napier jumped from the bow to get on the dock. When the boat moved away from the dock, her back legs were on the boat, and her front feet were on the dock, stretching her out until she fell in! She was much too heavy for me to pull her out by myself. Nikki was getting very concerned while George was just looking befuddled.

Napier had to be encouraged to swim to the boat ramp over a hundred yards away, which—being a strong swimmer—she did with ease. George was shaking his head. We unloaded, said thank you again and a final good-bye to George. As he was backing away from the marina, we yelled, "See you next year!" Now we had a wet, smelly dog to deal with on a long drive to Georgia, so Nikki got paper towels from the toilets to dry her off. The mayhem somehow made it easier not to dwell on the sadness of saying good-bye. After a slight delay, we were on our way, hoping to make the state line by 2:00 p.m.

We had made reservations at the Holiday Inn that accommodated pets, just past Tipton, Georgia, hoping to get there by five. It would then be a much easier drive to Blairsville the next day; that way, we could unload in the daylight.

The drive back home with a smelly dog was a little disconcerting; however, with windows open for fresh air, it made the situation tolerable. As we were chatting about our island experiences over the last several months, of finding new friends and entertaining old friends while discovering a new place together, it made the trip very enjoyable. It didn't seem that long before we were turning off the interstate to fill up with gas while Nikki walked the dog, then it was on to a drive-through survival station for burgers and fries. The smell of our salty four-legged friend was much better now, or maybe by that time, we were immune to it! As we drove on, the conversation turned to us planning that year's business trips to the United Kingdom, to see friends and relatives in and around Cambridgeshire and Suffolk, as well as staying in Newcastle with Julliet; we hoped that Jonathan would come down from Scotland.

We had so much to look forward to; it made leaving the island less sad than it could have been. Nikki and I were looking forward to being together in our personal lives, with a partnership in business and an enjoyable life full of travel throughout Europe and the Americas.

When you first step onto Little Gasparilla Island, you will find a treasure that buries itself deep in your soul and is yours forever; it becomes, my fellow islanders, an unbreakable bond between us.

EPILOGUE

W E SPENT ANOTHER two winters in Tom and Amber's beach house on LGI. The water never did get any better. Then we were lucky enough to find a much newer house toward the south end of the island to rent that backed onto Grande Avenue and that had much better water, as well as an extra bedroom and bathroom.

Nikki and I rented there for another seven years, keeping our very close ties to the folks on Peacock Lane. We also found many new friends on Gulf Street and Sea Grape Lane where they would dead end close to our new digs. Many more friends would visit us from Canada and Great Britain who were either childhood friends of Nikki or others we acquired as friends through living in and working in Great Britain during the 1980s and '90s, right up to 2007.

The last three of our winter stays on LGI were cut short by the scourge of red tide (more on this subject in a future book). The fish were floating ashore faster than we could bury them in their thousands. The stench on the beach and on the Bay was not only harmful to animals, but to humans as well.

We then bought a house in Hudson, Florida, where the wretched red tide seemed to hardly ever appear. The Hudson home was on a canal with views of the Gulf; this was to become our winter home until retirement. When we did retire from the antique business, LGI was still calling me to come back. After looking for a place to buy, Nikki definitely wanted to be on the mainland, so we compromised by buying in the area of Cape Haze in the golfing community of Windward, directly across the Bay from the island.

We brought our pontoon boat down from Hudson to moor at Eldred's Marina, so when the need to visit friends or go over and enjoy the solitude arose, it was easy to do.

George Geier, at the age of ninety-one, could no longer commute to LGI or stay by himself because of his ever-increasing lack of mobility due to a severe stroke. George passed away on Christmas Day 2006 at the age ninety-three in New Jersey.

As it turned out, it was most fortunate that Nikki and I did not buy a home on the island, as she was diagnosed with cancer in late December 2009 and needed the close proximity of doctors and hospitals. Nikki passed away in her much-loved home in Placida on February 21, 2011, with Julliet, Jonathan, and myself by her side.

George's daughter Meg has allowed Rosemary and me to stay in George's little round house this winter 2012/13 to finish the story. Even though George left the island in 2004, I feel he will always be here, and it is a real privilege for us to be able to use his house and have its energy guide us.

Lloyd's biography:

Lloyd Arthur Wiggins was born in Tampa Florida in 1946. He attended Riverview elementary and East Bayhigh school in Hillsborough County, Florida. In 1964 he volunteered to join the US Army and was stationed in Mannheim Germany. After a European discharge, he travelled to England for a year where he married Nikki Hinch. They lived in Florida and Lloyd worked for Delta Airlines from 1968-1981, then they emigrated to England and Scotland and started a successful antique exporting business, finally retiring to Placida, Florida in 2010.

Rosemary's biography:

Rosemary Egerton Letts was born in 1946 and grew up in the greater London area attending St. Andrew's school, Harrow College for girls and two technical colleges. She was an apprentice hairdresser in Harrods and married John Letts, a university graduate, in 1966. He was recruited by Boeing and they spent a year in Seattle. After returning home and having quintuplets in 1969, they immigrated to Vancouver Canada in 1974.She now divides her time between Vancouver Island and Placida Florida.

CPSIA information can be obtained
at www.ICGtesting.com
Printed in the USA
LVHW032346120720
660491LV00002B/359